CHRISTIAN LIFE
DAY BY DAY

D1392713

CHRISTIAN LIFE
DAY BY DAY

Talks to the Family

by

LEON JOSEPH CARDINAL SUENENS

Archbishop of Malines-Brussels

LONDON
BURNS & OATES

BURNS & OATES LIMITED
25 Ashley Place, London, S.W.1

This translation of
Vie quotidienne, Vie chrétienne (*Desclée de Brouwer*)
was made by S. F. L. TYE.

Catalogue No.: 5/4220

First published November 1963
Second impression March 1964
Third impression September 1964
Fourth impression September 1965
Fifth impression February 1967

PRINTED BY PHOTOLITHOGRAPHY IN GREAT BRITAIN BY
LATIMER TREND & CO. LTD.
WHITSTABLE

CONTENTS

CONTENTS

CONTENTS

I

LEARNING THAT GOD LOVES US

> *I have bought thee for myself, and given thee the name thou bearest: thou belongest to me.*—Isaias 43.1.

I WANT to talk to you about the fatherhood of God.

We all know that God is our Father. That is what we call him in the Lord's Prayer: "Our Father, who art in heaven." But are we really convinced that God is a Father, that "there is no Father like him", that all fatherhood proceeds from his and takes its title from it? Do we grasp all the meaning, all the warmth, all the fullness the word conveys? It is a question worth asking, because our faith in the paternal love of God is at the very heart of Christianity.

We Christians are so familiar with it all, so "settled", as Péguy put it, that we sometimes need to pay heed to our non-Catholic brethren to appreciate with a fresh mind the treasures of our faith.

Man, the contemptible atom?

The modern unbeliever finds it hard to accept this idea of the fatherhood of God. He is fascinated, disturbed by the picture painted by the scientists of man lost in the immensity of space, with his sputniks and artificial satellites beginning to hurtle across it in all directions. Modern man feels lost in this gigantic maze. He feels like a speck of dust, a drop of water in the ocean, an ant in an ant-hill. Knowing how small he is, he is tempted to believe that he has become too small, too insignificant for God to take any notice of him.

Listen to one of our contemporary atheists talking about the insignificance of man with no sense of destiny left, man with no father in heaven:

Man, a contemptible atom lost in the inert and unbounded cosmos, knows that his feverish activity is only a minor local phenomenon, without meaning and without purpose. He knows that his values are valid only for him, and that from the viewpoint of the stars, the fall of an empire or even the collapse of an ideal counts for no more than the destruction of an ant-hill by a heedless traveller's foot.

And so the only thing he can do is to try and forget the inhuman vastness which crushes him and which is indifferent to his existence. Rejecting the barren dizziness of the infinite, deaf to the terrifying silence of space, he can only force himself to become as self-centred as the universe is inhuman. Desperately thrown back on himself, humbled and earthbound, he will devote his energies to the realization of his puny plans or pretend to give them the same importance as if they were concerned with eternal realities.[1]

That is man, according to the rationalistic atheists. It is to man in this state, who has lost his sense of

[1] J. Rostand, *L'homme*.

God, that we have to reveal the loving presence of a father who cares for him as an individual.

God cares

It seems so incredible that God should bother about us or concern himself with the day-to-day running of the world. The world today holds three thousand million people, and before long, in a few years' time, it will be five thousand, six thousand million. Does God bother about each of these men, individually? Of course, we would admit that he is concerned with them as a whole, taking them altogether. A little like the head of a state who knows his people, not individually, but collectively. We believe, more or less unconsciously, that we get only a three-thousand-millionth part of God's attention, and that later on it will be a five-thousand-millionth part. . . .

This kind of arithmetic does not hold good when we are talking about God. He gives to each, not a tiny portion, but the whole of his care and his love.

We so seldom meet a man who really cares for other people, a man for whom they really exist, not as cogs in the wheel or numbers in a catalogue, but as beings in themselves, alive and inescapably individual. So seldom, but how wonderful when we do! It is a miracle, and God makes it come true for us all. To God, we exist. He gives his fatherly affection to each of us. Is this exaggeration or rhetoric? No: the truth, pure and simple.

God loves us. Christ gave his life for you and me, just as if we were the only people on earth.

Pascal's phrase in the *Pensées* (in the *Mémorial*), where he puts these words into the mouth of Jesus, "This is the drop of blood I shed for you," is often quoted with approval. This may be all very well in a literary work. But in reality, Christ shed *all* his blood for each one of us. This is something we must believe with a lively faith. We must believe in the personal love of God for each one of us.

The way God looks at us

When we are talking about God, we must reverse our usual way of looking at things. To God, the world we see, touch, feel, the world with its everyday happenings, its hustle and bustle that we read about in the newspapers, is a stage, a backcloth, a setting for life. What holds pride of place in God's interest is not peace treaties, changes in alliances, political upheavals. These things all have their importance, no doubt, on their own scale and on their own plane; but the first object of God's care and attention, his original centre of interest, is each man on earth, each human person, each immortal soul. "God," says Bergson, "created the world and turned it upside down just to make saints." That is the only reason for the world's existence. If the day came when the world ceased to give God what he was looking for, it would come to an end for lack of meaning. God turns the world upside down for his elect, for men, his friends, for each one of us. Sometimes this providence of God is so striking that even our eyes can perceive it.

Scripture tells us that in the days of Caesar

Augustus, when Quirinus was governor of Syria, a census was ordered of all the inhabitants of the Roman Empire. This decree of the emperor sent large numbers of men and women on the move to the census offices. If we look for the main reason for these mass movements up and down the country, if we look at these crowds as God looks at them, we see that his eyes followed with special attention a woman called Mary and her husband, Joseph. We shall see that his Providence was guiding them through all this human activity towards the place where the Messiah was to be born, to Bethlehem.

We might say that, in the example I have given, the love of God was clearly seen because he was making preparations for the birth of his own Son. But we should be wrong. No doubt divine intervention is more strikingly evident in this case: but the more we are united to his Son, the more we are brothers of Christ and sons of the same Father, the more this personal exercise of providence will come into play in all our lives and in the day-to-day pattern of our existence. This is a point to which I shall return later.

For the moment, I simply ask you to open your hearts to God's welcome, to his fatherly love for each one of you; and I ask you to say this to him: "Father, I trust in your love for me." May this trust open your heart to joy, that joy which the world cannot give, but which it will never be able to take away from you.

II

LEARNING TO BELIEVE IN GOD'S HIDDEN LOVE

It is not for thee to know, now, what I am doing; but thou wilt understand it afterwards.—
Jesus to St Peter (John 13. 7).

Omnipresent love

As I was saying, God loves us. He loves us individually, one by one. It is good to be aware of this direct and all-embracing love of God. We do not remain impersonal before him. Intimate knowledge, mutual affection, serious conversation are the bonds which bind a father to his children.

God knows us one by one. He does not get one mixed up with another.

He knows us by name, and our first name.

He knows the story of our life, page by page.

He knows every line of it, everything written between the lines; even the watermark on the paper.

He follows us step by step, from the cradle to the grave. Nothing escapes his notice, his tenderness; not a hair of our head can fall without his permission.

The Master said: "My sheep are known to me and know me" (John 10. 14). Even in the Old Testament, the Lord expressed his love for men in the words: "What, can a woman forget her child . . .? Let her forget; I will not be forgetful of thee" (Isaias 49. 15).

14

It was this that caused St Francis de Sales to say that, on the day of judgment, he would rather be judged by God than by his own mother.

God loves us; he knows everything; he understands. It is so good to be perfectly understood, according to the best that is in us. And so unusual! "You have to be so much with me to be my friend," wrote Bloy in his *Journal*. God is so much with us, by our side, at our elbow. He is prejudiced in our favour. He takes the first step towards forgiveness at the least sign of good will on our part, and even that is the result of his grace at work in us.

In the Gospel parable, it is the father who sets out to meet the prodigal son as soon as he sees him on the distant horizon. He gives him no time to put his repentance into words. His arms are already open, and the reconciliation is complete before the penitent starts on the *Confiteor*.

God loves us and keeps us in all our ways.

Scripture tells us that he has given his angels charge over us to watch over us. As it says elsewhere, God has counted all our bones.

Hidden love

But his love remains hidden.

When the disciples saw Christ walking on the waters of the lake, they thought he was a ghost.

On Easter morning, when Mary Magdalen saw the Master in the Garden of Olives, she thought he was the gardener.

When the disciples met him on the road to Emmaus,

they thought he was a stranger who had no concern with all they had been hoping for.

The ways of God are not generally understood. Faith, an awakened faith, is needed to perceive them.

God keeps himself in hiding. But he is there, concealed in chance happenings and unexpected encounters. It is a good thing to look for him, beneath the externals, behind the appearances. Sometimes these chance happenings are so illuminating that we cannot help seeing the Lord quite clearly.

Everyone will have had some experience of this in the course of his life. A particular meeting, a book, a word heard by chance, a trial we had to bear have been God in disguise for us, God was there; hidden, silent, but so very much present.

A spiritual writer once said:

"If a soul needs the presence of a particular adviser to say the right word to him, God will send that person from the ends of the earth."

God may be hidden in a wireless wave, a picture on the cinema screen, the reflection of a passer-by: "Would you but listen to his voice today!" says the Scripture. "Do not harden your hearts" (Psalm 94. 8).

Coincidence: God in disguise

God loves us with a personal, direct, all-embracing love, which is concealed by the action of chance and secondary causes. There are some surprising coincidences in the Gospels.

Take our Lord, tired after his journey, sitting by the well—Jacob's well. What could be more natural? A

Samaritan woman comes along with a water-pot. What could be more simple? And yet, what an encounter between the mercy of God and the weakness of man! On that conversation with the Master the whole destiny of the woman is staked: he rescues her from her past and makes her the messenger of the Messiah among her own people.

Take Cana, for example, the wedding Jesus went to with his mother. At a certain moment, the wine threatens to run short. Mary makes a simple request to her son: "They have no wine left" (John 2. 3). And the first public miracle Jesus did was the answer to this request; a miracle provoked by a trifle, a mere detail of housekeeping; a miracle worked to prevent embarrassment to simple people who at this stage may not yet have noticed that there was anything wrong. God thought it was worth the trouble of taking notice of this trifling incident to be an instrument of his omnipotence and love.

Take Nathanael, coming to the Master at the time when Jesus is recruiting his first disciples. Jesus says of him, when he sees him coming: "Here comes one who belongs to the true Israel; there is no falsehood in him" (John 1. 47).

"How dost thou know me?" Nathanael asks.

Jesus answers him: "I saw thee when thou wast under the fig-tree, before Philip called thee."

We do not know what Jesus was referring to, but his reply is an example of that Providence of God which nothing escapes. No more than the widow's mite escaped it, when she put a farthing into the treasury. No more than the movements of that young man from Jerusalem escaped it, when he was carrying a jar of water on the way out of town and was indicated by the Master to John and Peter as the one they had to follow when they went to make their preparations for the paschal meal. No, nothing is too small; to his eyes, everything has a meaning, a purpose, a significance. He knows all our deeds and actions; he follows and motivates them, and this immense action of Providence serves to weave the fabric of our life and bind all the threads together.

There are times when the Providence of God makes a startling impact on our lives. And sometimes the circumstances surrounding the death of someone who is leaving this world make it very apparent. "Life," says one philosopher, "is a sentence we don't understand the meaning of until the last word has been spoken." The last moment of a life is at times marked by something that simply forces us to see the hand of God in it, the tender love of God calling his servant to himself.

I think of Father Sertillanges, found dead at his desk at a time when he was preaching a retreat for children. He had just finished writing out the notes for his next talk with the words: "Let us all prepare, in this way, to meet in heaven." The ink on the word "heaven" was still not dry when they found him, asleep in the Lord.

I think, too, of a certain great Benedictine who devoted his life to extolling the mystery of Easter and who died in church, in choir, on Holy Saturday, at the very moment when they had finished intoning the *Exsultet*.

It has been truly said: "Souls and chance happenings correspond." What is there surprising about that, since it is the same love of God which inspires them and brings about the encounter?

It is good for us to take note of this all-pervading Providence and open our hearts to welcome it.

To help us recognize this presence of God in human life it is important to take into account the special law which governs the action of God in the world and which we always tend to overlook.

God's time

We think God is absent, that he has left us to our fate, because he does not make his appearance at the moment we have chosen.

Now it is for God, not for us, to decide the "times and seasons". And the Scriptures tell us again and again how insistent God is on choosing his own time.

How often Jesus said: "My time has not yet come," or "The time is coming. . . ." Clearly, he allowed no one, except his Father, to decide which was God's time. He did not wish to be coerced or rushed. He knew how to bide his time and choose the right moment.

When the storm came on, he was asleep in the boat. He was in no hurry to come to the rescue of his terrified disciples. But he was there all right, and he was ready to give the sign which calmed the waves when the time came.

When his disciples questioned him about the future, he told them: "the day of it and the hour of it are unknown to you" (Matt. 25. 13). And he shared his secret with no one.

To Peter, who failed to understand why the Master should want to wash his feet, he said: "It is not for thee to know, now, what I am doing; but thou wilt understand it afterwards."

We, too, must wait for the sign of God's love until the time he has appointed for it. We must accept God's own rhythm. It is because they want to impose their own rhythm on God that Christians are so apt to complain that God does not answer their prayers. He does answer them, without fail. But in his own time. "Not mine," says the Lord, "to think as you think, deal as you deal" (Isaias 55. 8). Leave it to him: he knows, infinitely better than we do, what he is doing. And let us believe, with unshakeable faith, that "everything helps to secure the good of those who love God" (Rom. 8. 28).

The love of God makes light of apparent obstacles or barriers. Give him your trust, your confidence. One day you will thank God, in heaven, for the prayers he has answered here on earth, not in your way, but in his. One day you will thank God for having loved you in the way God does love, with all the height, all the breadth, all the depth of a love which passes human understanding and overwhelms us. Then, the whole of eternity will not be too long for us to say "thank you".

III

LEARNING TO KEEP IN TOUCH WITH GOD

Live on, then, in my love.—
Jesus to his apostles (John 15. 9).

WE like to look forward in imagination to life's great moments for a chance of displaying courage and heroism, yet we let a thousand and one ordinary, everyday opportunities of doing humble, but praiseworthy, services slip by unheeded.

Communion under all kinds

We must learn to act big in little things, to make our lives a continual communion with God through all the different unrecorded events of our lives, throughout the humdrum existence of every day.

"O my God," wrote one spiritual writer, "if I am to love you *above all things,* give me a chance of loving you each day *above one thing.*" That's the way it's done.

Holiness is not a matter of striking deeds. It lies in doing what is asked of us with a good heart, doing what is within reach, doing the things we pass over as insignificant or ordinary.

The language of Christian life is prose, not poetry. It is composed of the drabness of our everyday occupations. But we must get used to seeing the will of God

21

in the most ordinary happenings. What we call a "turn of events" is the hand of God controlling and guiding things. God has many ways of making his presence felt, and Christians must make use of them all to keep in touch with him.

We are accustomed to enter into communion with God under the form of bread and wine. We know, by faith, that as soon as the sacred words: "This is my body, this is my blood" have been pronounced, Christ is present. We know that Christ is present in his entirety in the host and in each fragment of the host, however small. This is the mystery of the sacramental presence, which passes human understanding, but which we accept from the lips of God with gratitude and reverence. This is the first method of entering into communion. There are others.

When I accept the will of God with regard to myself, my life and every detail of my life, just as it comes, with all its limitations and frustrations, I am entering into communion with God: not, this time, a eucharistic communion, but a vital communion which lasts all day, all my life.

What our Lord asks me to do is to unite myself with him, hour by hour, minute by minute, by doing, at every single moment, his most holy will.

What is required of a watch is that its hands should keep their appointed time, that at any particular moment they should be exactly where their maker intended them to be. In terms of man, this means obedience to the will of God, concentration on the present moment, sanctity in little things.

There is a constant temptation to live in a different period of time from the one God wants us to live in. The young live in the future; they are full of plans, all relating to tomorrow. The old look back, trying to live in the past, and the past becomes more and more present to them. Only a few live in the present, the "glorious present". Only a few seek out the will of God in every moment of passing time, where it lies hidden as truly as in every fragment of the host on the altar. They can see and adore the divine will in its entirety in every detail of human life.

To be in touch with God in the midst of life means that the eye of faith sees beyond appearances and discovers God in the daily round. God is always ready to come to us in disguise at the most unexpected moments.

We read in the life of St Gertrude that the saint used to experience ecstasies on occasions which we should not have thought solemn enough to justify it. One day, St Gertrude was late in arriving at the refectory and opened a cupboard to look for some bread. At that very moment, she was seized and penetrated by the grace of God.

The material of holiness is not some rare substance, like Carara marble, hard to come by. No, the stones we find by the wayside are good enough. But we have to ignore the effect of secondary causes and discover God beyond them.

Suppose some happiness comes my way. I can look no further than the immediate cause and continue on my journey. Or I can go back to the ultimate cause, which is no less than God, God's smile, God's encouragement, beckoning to us to go on, urging us to do better. God lies hidden in all human joys, great or small. Heaven is revealed in any passing glimpse of the spiritual and God's presence in man's brief moment of contact with the divine.

Communion through suffering

We must also learn to keep in union with God through suffering. That is not so easy. The human cause of the evil which attacks and wounds us too easily absorbs our attention. Yet God lies hidden in the heart of suffering. When suffering is accepted, he works miracles of redemption at its very heart, miracles of purification and detachment which pave the way for increase of grace.

This communion with the Lord in suffering was once expressed by a soul very closely united with God in these words, which are a cry of faith and a light in the darkness:

My God, let me see you at work everywhere, in every creature who wounds me, in everything which happens to upset me, as well as in everything which fills me with joy. Let me learn by experience that even if the secondary causes are infinitely varied, the first cause is always the same, and that cause, O Lord, is you! The hand is the same, even if the glove changes. It wears a velvet, horse-hair or iron glove, according to the consolation or affliction I feel when it touches me. God, my God, it is always your dear and tender hand that presses mine to say: "I love you." But however soft the hand, it is hard and cold if not painful when it squeezes mine with an iron glove.... The horse-hair glove is, to say the least of it, trying.... We should like to feel nothing but the velvet glove all the time, but that's the one you wear, Lord, perhaps least of all.... Do what you like, my Master, don't bother about me. Put on whichever glove you like, squeeze as much as you like. Only give me leave, as your child, to take off your glove and kiss your hand.

Such is the language of faith. We must all see beyond appearances. Faith is like radar, perceiving objects through fog and darkness. Who can fail to marvel at the scientific discovery which enables a plane to go on through the darkness? Faith likewise penetrates the veils, the appearances. It is a sort of X-ray that sees what is there, in spite of the opaqueness. May faith increase in each one of us, give us eyes to see what is real and help us to make our lives a permanent state of communion with God.

Let us not live in dreams, let us not fall back on alibis, nor wait for tomorrow or the next day to make our lives worth while. Now is the time, this very moment, that the Master has fixed for our meeting; and he is waiting for us: "See where I stand at the door, knocking" (Apoc. 3. 20). That is what the Lord has to say to each one of us.

Let us ask him into our life, as into a room ready

for him. Let him put everything in its proper place and keep the place of honour for him. That will be the most wonderful communion of all. It is always within our reach.

IV

LEARNING TO LISTEN

*Listen, then, my son, and shew
thyself wise, keeping still an
even course.*—Proverbs 23. 19.

IF we are going to open our hearts to others, there is
one quality we shall have to acquire, and this may
be more difficult than we think. We shall have to learn
to listen. Very few men and women know how to
listen properly. The majority of conversations between
human beings are interrupted monologues, cutting
across each other.

Monologues or dialogues

When people meet, they usually start by asking:
"How are you?", "How are things?" But who stops to
listen to the answer? In England people say: "How
do you do?" so automatically that it is now bad form
to start explaining how you feel. It is just a matter of
form, a mere convention. After this, the man who
started the conversation will usually begin to talk
about himself and his affairs, going into innumer-
able details. At a certain moment, the man to whom
he is talking will seize on one of these details in mid-
speech and attach a story of his own to it or something
he wants to talk about. From then on, each will follow
his own course, only pausing to take breath, like a car

stopping at the traffic lights; and each of them takes the whole procedure for granted so long as he continues to have his own say. A caricature? I don't think so. You can find plenty of examples of it at all levels of society.

Not many people listen to others. People don't seem to realize that they have two ears and one mouth, and that nature herself expects them to listen twice as often as they speak. The reason for this is that every one is so full of his own affairs that there is no room for anybody else's. This is one gift we have to acquire: the art of listening. The saints, now, were good at listening. A man like the Curé d'Ars knew, in spite of his sixteen hours a day in the confessional, how to listen to his penitents, and they all left the box amazed at the personal attention they had received. Sometimes you hear it said of someone: "He listens to you as if he had nothing else to do." That is a wonderful gift, and it has a tremendous effect. For nothing opens the heart more than complete attention, taking the trouble to enter into the worries which are being put before you. A school of patience, but, in the first place, a school of self-forgetfulness!

Listening to more than the words

You have to listen, not just to what is said, but also to what is not said. Not many people can take in the meaning of an awkward silence, a half-uttered word, a word kept back. They listen to words and sounds; they have no ears for mute distress or semi-confidences timidly offered. Sometimes you even have to arrive at a meaning when the words say the opposite, like Our Lady at the marriage at Cana, when she asked the Master to do something and received an apparently negative reply. She turned to the servants and made a sign to them to be ready for what was coming. She listened to more than the words.

You have to listen, even when you know more, perhaps, about the matter than the man who is speaking to you.

You have to listen by raising to the highest possible level the value of what others have to contribute. Do you remember what Lavelle said? "The greatest good we can do for others is not to give them what we have, but to show them how much they have to give."

There are wonderful listeners who have the gift of getting others to talk, bringing out the best in them, making them surpass themselves by encouragement and expectation. Such listeners are rare, but history tells us that more than one writer found the best of his inspiration and power to write in the affection and comradeship of a wife eager for communion with her husband.

Blessed are they who know how to listen intently enough to hear God. We find it difficult to believe that God speaks to us, yet he never stops speaking. Then why don't we hear his voice? Simply because we are not listening. If the radio is not switched on, no music can be heard in the room. Yet the room is full of music; all we have to do is tune in. We should tune in to the voice of God, who speaks to us in the Scriptures and in life, in miracles and acts of Providence. But to hear God himself in the midst of all the noise we make, when all the interference is jamming his speech, we must tune in to his own particular wave-length, which he makes known to those who pray to him and listen to him in silence.

V

LEARNING TO ADORE

> *They ... fell down to worship him;*
> *and, opening their store of treasures,*
> *they offered him gifts, of gold and*
> *frankincense and myrrh.*—Matt. 2. 11.

AT Christmas time we are called upon to fall on our knees before the mystery of God's love, which passes human understanding. That God should love us, we can understand. But that his love should have gone to such lengths, even to the crib, that is amazing. A love which crosses barriers like that is out of this world. Faced with love like that, there is only one attitude to take, the attitude of Mary and Joseph, the shepherds on Christmas Day and the three kings later on, the attitude of Christian people throughout the ages—adoration. Such depths of love, such folly—God becoming incarnate—baffle man's understanding. "Anything else, but not that," the unbeliever will say. Faced by the crib, man finds himself at the crossroads. Either he accepts God and the mystery of his love, or he denies it.

Mystery or absurdity?

If he chooses God, he accepts the mystery at the same time. It is natural that God should be infinitely above man. It is normal that his ways should be shrouded in mystery. If man understood God, God would cease to be God, since to understand is to be equal, and man would cease to be man. It is natural for man, in his state, to kneel before something greater than himself. If on the other hand he denies God, he chooses absurdity and chaos. Life is no more than a flash of light between two voids. And putting the relative end to end or multiplying the contingent by the contingent will not lead to the discovery of the absolute and the necessary.

The earth does not contain within itself the reason for its own existence. Each part of it may cease to exist. To try and account for it by the simple juxtaposition of each of its parts is to choose nonsense.

God, or a vacuum; the mystery of God, or chaos. There is only one choice open to us. The only thing to do, if we want to be fully reasonable and clearheaded is to fall on our knees.

The duty of adoration

Christmas is first and foremost the feast of adoration. It is so seldom that men really adore God. When they pray, it is usually to beg for something or to pour out their complaints to God. Prayer is too often an activity which makes them concentrate on themselves instead of opening their hearts. If we had invented the Our Father, we should have reversed the petitions, and we should have started like this: "Our Father, who art in heaven, give us this day our daily bread and deliver us from evil." And then, perhaps, we might have prayed that God's will should be done and his kingdom come: but that is not so certain.

Man's first duty to God is to acknowledge him for what he is, to treat him as he deserves to be treated, as God, as infinite.

It is a great thing to see a man on his knees before God. Such a man, adoring God, is in his proper place. He has a sense of balance and proportion. He is affirming that he is nothing and that God is everything. That is the simple truth; it is only just. Adoration is the first step to all real prayer.

The family at prayer

But we should not be alone in our adoration. "Come," the shepherds said to each other, "let us adore the Lord." The liturgy repeats the invitation. We must kneel round the crib together. The family circle is the place where we should perform this solemn duty.

Does family prayer have a place at your fireside?

It is a great sight and a lovely one—to see a family at prayer; a home where, at evening time, when the day's work is done, they get together, before they say goodnight, and say their prayers together. Those voices which blend together, from the faltering tones of the youngest to father's deeper and more serious voice, are a sign of hearts and minds blended into one, the secret of the happy home. Father Peyton's magnificent campaign for the family rosary and the slogan he has blazoned throughout the five continents—*the family that prays together stays together*—are well known. It is so true. Prayer is the cement that binds the members of the family one to another. It gives birth to affection, loyalty and love.

2

The "Gloria in excelsis"

We ought to pray together. And why not sing to-gether? And isn't singing a part of Christmas? It was the song the angels sang that told the shepherds that something incredible was going to happen. This song Christendom has made its hymn, its own: *Glory be to God, to God on high and on earth. Peace to men of good will,* and it has been repeated from age to age.

How can we help thinking of her who handed them down to us? For how do we know that these words greeted our Saviour's birth? It was not the shepherds who told the evangelists about them, for they had no contact with them. It was not St Joseph, for he was dead by the time the Master chose his apostles.

These words, like the other wonderful things St Luke tells us about, lay hidden in the heart of Mary, who "kept in her heart the memory of all this" (Luke 2. 51). The *Gloria* was the song of the angels, and Mary's secret song, before it was ours. We ought to recapture its joy and magnificence in company with them and her.

We don't sing the old carols often enough nowadays, or the modern ones either. It would be a good thing if we had some gramophone records at home to play according to the season of the liturgical year, so that we could live the great joyful festivals of the Church together in unison. The liturgy should be extended into the bosom of the family. The song of the Church ought to go on resounding in the atmosphere of our homes; the lights on the altar will burn less brightly, no doubt, but just as truly, in the home, and everybody should feel that it's Christmas everywhere and be able to see the joy of it on everybody's face.

What a holy feast Christmas is! May it mark for each one of us a renewal of our inmost Christian life. May it bring to all the realization of the link between the two phrases: *glory to God* and *peace to men of good will*. Peace will grow among men with the glory they give to God. The glory of God is the very peace of men. By kneeling together on this Christmas night before God who became one of us, we perform the most direct, the most constructive and the most creative act of human brotherhood.

VI

LEARNING TO SAY "THANK YOU"

We give thanks to God always . . .—
St Paul (1 Thess. 1. 2).

Two words are reckoned among the finest in man's vocabulary; two very short words, but if you think about it, they go a long way: the words "yes" and "thank you". When you think how rare gratitude is, it looks as though men find it very hard to say "thank you". And yet it would make so much difference to human relations if we understood more clearly our duty of showing gratitude.

Our Lord drew attention to this serious failing in the Gospels. Do you remember the story of the ten lepers who were made clean? Our Lord performed the miracle; they went away happy and pleased. Only one of the lepers thought of going back to say "thank you" to the Master. "And the other nine," asked Jesus, "where are they?" (Luke 17. 17). They had simply forgotten to say "thank you".

Thanking others

Do we realize how much we take for granted the things people do for us, as if they were something due to us? Doesn't it often happen that when an employer's attention is drawn to the devoted work of an employee, or a master to a servant's, you get the

36

reply: "But that is what they are paid for." They pay up and think that's the end of that.

It is worth reflecting what a wealth of Christian charity and human warmth there is in a "thank you", even when the service has been paid for. Besides, there are so many things which are paid for, not by money, but by a smile, some mark of attention, or a "thank you". The florists have thought up a slogan: "Say it with flowers." We ought to be able to find other ways of expressing our feelings than paying money or even giving tips. There are some human feelings which are expressed by a gesture which costs nothing, but which nothing else can replace. The happiness of a family depends largely on this duty of saying "thank you" to each other.

Happy the home where the children have learned to say "thank you" to their mother and father who make sacrifices for them and work for their well-being all day long. It is one of those things that go without saying, but it goes much better if it is said. There is an art in saying "thank you" at the right time and in the right way, and it has to be learned. Life is made up of a series of little things and to a great extent family happiness depends on them. One of these little things is a "thank you" said at the right moment.

The husband's "thank you" to his wife is worth all the money in the world. It shows her that her husband notices what she does for him, that he appreciates the love and effort which go into the smallest details of daily life.

The wife's "thank you" to her husband is all and more than he needs to give him courage to take up daily his monotonous and tiring job and face the struggle for existence, in which the knocks are sometimes so hard and the antagonists so unscrupulous. It is a ray of sunshine that he takes with him into the drabness of his office or workshop. And man needs sunshine even more than bread.

And the manager's thanks to the man who works under him: what wonders that can work! It shows scant understanding of the social question to imagine that the conflict between management and workers is primarily a question of money. It is first and foremost a matter of human relations.

We are reminded of the miner who was questioned by King Albert of Belgium when he was going down a coal-mine. The king asked him if there was anything he wanted for himself and his comrades. "Sire," the reply came, proud and unhesitating, "we want people to respect us."

That was a cry from the heart. What men want most of all is respect, and gratitude is a sign of respect. That is why it touches the human heart so deeply.

We must learn to thank those in whose midst we live; our near and dear ones, to begin with. There is a danger of forgetting them, if we are not careful. From time to time we must pause, stand back a little and say the words which are too often left to be understood, but ought to be spoken aloud from time to time. The words "thank you" are among them.

Thanking God

It is also vital that we should learn to thank God. What for? For being God, in the first place. That is the great prayer of thanks where he is concerned. "We give you thanks," says the *Gloria* of the Mass, "for your great glory." Thanking God for being God, in communion with his own joy. Charles de Foucauld expressed his gratitude in the midst of his suffering and his personal crosses by saying to God those words, which are an expression of adoration in its purest form and which put everything into perspective: "My God, your happiness is enough for me." That kind of thanks is theological charity in its most profound form.

We must also thank God for everything we owe him. Here we have a permanent motive for joy and gratitude. We can never finish counting our blessings. Let it suffice to say that we must thank God for being our Father, for we have the joy of being in all truth his children. We are divine by naturalization, sons by adoption.

And we must thank God for being our Brother, for having become one of us, so that in him and through him we might enter the divine family with full rights and a whole share.

And we must thank God for being sanctified by the Holy Spirit, the "sanctifier and life-giver", who wants to make us penetrate into the very depths of God and associate us with the power of his love.

We must learn to thank him for every object he has put at our disposal: for the roof which shelters us, this table, this bed, this armchair, these books, this lamp which is burning, this fire which warms us, the friends whom life places in our path, and the thousands and thousands of other things within reach of my hands. It is God who, by means of secondary causes, has given them to us. It is to him, as the supreme cause of all our well-being, that we should show gratitude.

It is often interesting and illuminating to listen to the last earthly words of some chosen soul as they are spoken. Sometimes they give meaning to a whole life and open up a window on the spirituality which inspired them. Do you know the last words of St Clare, that fresh and pure soul whose life was such a noble echo of the Gospel? Feeling that death was near, she turned to God in a final prayer and was heard to murmur these words: "Thank you, Lord, for having created me."

This is the highest thanks a creature owes to his creator. It is the cry of a soul which understands the splendour of gratitude.

VII

LEARNING TO BE SILENT

But Jesus still would not answer him, so that Pilate was full of astonishment.—Mark 15. 5.

The vision at Nazareth

Was the Holy Family a silent family, a home of pure contemplation, or was it an ordinary home where speech alternated with silence, prayer with conversation and work with leisure? Everything goes to show that it was typical of the normal, ordinary home where speech and silence have their place. Yet it is silence that strikes us first.

Mary hears from the archangel the most momentous news: the Annunciation. The conversation is brief. One essential question: "How can that be?" A reply: "Let it be unto me according to thy word." Then, silence in face of the whole world, even Joseph, out of respect for a mystery which is beyond her and which she leaves in the hands of God.

Elsewhere in the Scriptures we learn that Mary kept the words she had heard and the joys she had lived through in the silence of her heart.

There is virtue in silence just as there is virtue in speech. The two virtues are to be practised in turn, according to the varying need for one or the other. In the Church, too, there are silent orders: the

Carmelites, the Carthusians, the Trappists. They continue the great tradition of the silent, contemplative life. Side by side with them are active orders, proclaiming with loud and vigorous voice the message of God which the Gospel bids us shout from the housetops. Complementary vocations, both magnificent. It is the silence of the contemplatives that gives sustenance to the words of the apostles. It is in the silence of the hill-tops that the torrents find their source; from them they pour down into the valley and water the plain.

Something of the same sort must come about in every Christian home. We must all learn when to speak and when to be silent. We must learn to mix the two in their proper proportions.

Silence which purifies

Let us talk about the virtue of silence.

Keep silent, particularly about anything which may destroy the peace and harmony of the family circle. It is so tempting to repeat some piquant and wounding phrase. It is so diverting to become a scandalmonger, a hawker of petty gossip which lightens the daily round in markets, clubs and drawing-rooms.

From time to time, there is a lot of talk about forming an anti-noise league. But there ought to be an anti-whispering league, a league against all the gossip that destroys justice and love among men. People do not take care to avoid the terrible evil of slander. It is so much the done thing to speak ill of one's neighbour! It is the thing that holds the conversation together, so much so that you have to make a special point of putting yourself on your guard against this subtle and insidious sin. What a contagious virus it is, and what a great deal of destruction it has to its credit! It is such a temptation to throw out a witty remark that strikes at the heart like a poisoned arrow. It is such a temptation to repeat it in conversation and score a cheap success.

Let us begin right away by cutting out of our conversation anything that keeps men apart, anything that makes them strangers to each other, anything that makes a barrier between them and exaggerates their differences and divergences. Let us make a resolution not to play the part of a broadcasting station when we hear news of some word or deed disparaging to our neighbour.

And let us stifle on our lips, and on our children's lips, the unkind, ironic, haughty and wounding word. "Do not judge others," said the Master (Matt. 7. 1), it is no business of yours. And to ensure that there should be no misunderstanding, he went on to say that God would judge us as we judged others. Do not judge, do not pass on tales. Cut off the current of calumny as it flows. What a fine short-circuit that would make! If every Christian played his part in this crusade of purely negative charity, merely by cutting these things out, the face of the world would change. How much healthier the atmosphere would become if we all kept to ourselves the slanders we heard or caught on the wing. All these treacherous tales are like noxious insects which fly off and carry infection elsewhere. Someone may object: "How do you expect us to kill the flies? There are too many of them." In a country as vast as China, the Communists, it seems, have succeeded, by waging an unrelenting campaign against the flies which used to infest it, in exterminating them. It is a matter of personal discipline and, where necessary, social charity. Their example will, I hope, inspire us to declare war, with plenty of pest-killer, on that verbal infection I am deploring, so that the world we live in can be made fit to breathe in.

It is not enough merely to avoid all that upsets good relations between people. We must also give positive encouragement to everything that brings them together.

Effort towards reconciliation

What we have to do is to look for the things that unite men, seek out the common stock of good will among men. Let us recall Marshal Lyautey's words:

I think [he said] that more often than we realize there exists a common denominator between men. It's like a blackboard. You chalk up huge fractions which seem impossible to simplify, but you know the arithmetical processes, the successive cancelling-out by which you arrive at the common denominator, a small, simple figure which could not have been foreseen in all those complicated workings. Perhaps I'm an optimistic type, but it seems to me that in all the things that divide men, we ought to find it easy to arrive at the common denominator.

Whether it is easy or not, we must be instruments of union between men. We must ask for the gift of becoming peacemakers. This is a grace the Blessed Virgin will gladly give to anyone who asks for it, for it is one of the most direct results of spiritual contact with her. Mary has a mother's heart for men, her children. And there is a delicate touch about a mother's love, a refinement in her tenderness, and tact, which makes her conceal her children's faults. The more our hearts are one with hers, the more we shall hide the faults of others; or, if we are obliged to reveal them, we shall suppress the name of the guilty party; or if we cannot avoid the duty of making it public, mention only those faults which have to be mentioned, no more, nothing else; always saying as little as possible, in imitation of the surgeon who cuts into the flesh only as much as necessary and never makes an incision wider or deeper than is needed.

Let us make the courageous resolution to bring men together instead of dividing them, eliminate from our vocabulary and conversation all that can hurt or wound our neighbour, so that there may descend on our earth a little of that peace God has promised to men of good will.

VIII

LEARNING TO TAKE RISKS

> *... so widely has my imprisonment become*
> *known, in Christ's honour, throughout the*
> *praetorium and to all the world beyond.*
> *And most of the brethren, deriving fresh*
> *confidence in the Lord from my imprisonment,*
> *are making bold to preach God's word with*
> *more freedom than ever.*—St Paul (Philippians 1. 13-14).

MODERN life is based more and more on the elimination of risk. Everything is calculated, worked out, insured against. How many people are hypnotized, once they go out into the world, by the prospect, not of final rest, which is less attractive to them, but of pre-final rest, the age of retirement and a pension. It needs more courage today than formerly to build one's life on any value but security and to dare to base one's existence on reasons for living greater than oneself.

Human courage

And yet life is not worth living unless it is dedicated to the service of values which transcend human life.

Man is not made for life on the ground floor, for a drab existence. His heart has more dimensions than the four walls of a house, however cosy and homely it may be. The human heart must have its reasons for living, reasons which measure up to its hunger and thirst. And the heart of man dreams of the infinite and the eternal. It dreams of giving itself to something beyond and outside itself.

This is true even in the present life. It is always a matter for astonishment to see how many people volunteer for tasks which call for heroism. When the Americans or the Russians want candidates for space flights, their only problem is the number they have to choose from. These young men, even young women, are not disillusioned with life; for the most part, they are people who long to risk their lives for something worth while.

A London newspaper once published this advertisement asking for volunteers to serve with an Antarctic expedition:

> Men wanted for dangerous expedition. Low pay, intense cold, months of total darkness, constant danger. Return uncertain. If successful, honour and gratitude.

There were five thousand replies to this advertisement from men who wanted to go with the expedition.

Let us salute their courage. But in this case it was primarily a question of physical courage. True moral courage is rarer in this base world. The courage to do one's duty, to go against the current and the prevailing wind, to brave irony and ridicule—St Peter, who trembled at a servant-girl's mockery at the praetorium realized something of it—this is what we must constantly strive for: courage in the face of life; courage to accept life.

Péguy speaks of the fathers of today as the great adventurers of the modern world. It is a great and wonderful thing to collaborate with God and do it with loyalty and generosity. It is a great and wonderful thing also on the part of parents, when the time comes for their children to choose their careers, not to stifle their youthful generosity and idealism, not to clip their wings with too much prudence.

The Christian risk

There is a magnificent Christian risk inherent in every human vocation. The young feel it by instinct: they must be allowed to run the risk of making something of their lives. This drive is often weakened by a cautious attitude. By coddling the young, we turn them into egoists. And egoism will take its revenge, sooner or later, on those whose love has failed to come up to the mark. I am thinking of the tragedy of so many vocations to a generous life, to the priesthood or the convent, which have been stifled by affection which was really only self-seeking, counsels of prudence which were really no more than a way of steering a human life off the track, back to a low level of aspiration.

Parents, think about this seriously. Sometimes, when young people get out of hand and want to follow mere caprice or impulse, you are justified in opposing them. But sometimes your opposition is a revolt against the Holy Spirit at work in the souls of your children, an obstacle to the grace of God. Your children are not your property. They belong to God, and he entrusts them to you. It is in the name of the Lord that I am here to plead their cause, the cause of God's rights, the cause of his love for your children.

What God longs for, what he wants for each of his children, is to develop the whole of his life, his power as Saviour of the world, in them. He wants to love the men of the twentieth century in them and through them, and so prepare them for their eternal destiny. God longs to make saints of all the beings he has created. We have no right to stand in the way of their true happiness.

The motive of profit cannot by itself be the response to a question so fundamental as the choice and direction of life. We have only one life. We are not fitted with a spare soul. We are not given one soul after another. It is a question of living a life which is worth something, worth something to our own family, no doubt, but also worth something to society at large. It is a question of giving one's life for others, of risking it in their service. This social, communal outlook is the only one which fits in with the demands of Christianity. From the Gospel point of view, there is no difference between social Christianity and the other kind. The social dimension is an integral and fundamental part of the Christian vocation. When I say this, dear parents, I am thinking of your older sons and daughters who find themselves at the crossroads.

Beware of too much prudence and caution. Help them to make a good start on the way.

The letter of the Gospel

But I am thinking of you, too. There is an element

of risk which you must preserve in your life, if you want it to be great and worth while. You must have the courage to take certain passages in the Gospels literally. You must have the courage to go beyond what is guaranteed solely by fleeting human wisdom.

Make a brief examination of conscience occasionally on this one point: "Do I ever do anything in my life which I should not have done if Christ had not come on earth?" Is there anywhere in your life a deed which, without him, you would not have done? If your life rolls on, from morning till night, with nothing unforeseen, if everything about you, twenty-four hours out of the twenty-four, can be explained in human terms, then Christianity has not penetrated you to your very depths.

Will you take a risk in the name of Jesus and for his sake? He is watching you; he is waiting for you. And he measures your heart's real love by the impulse which gets you out of yourself and makes you rebel against conformity. Have no fear: stop hugging the shore and make for the open sea. There is no need to be afraid of imitating St Peter occasionally and walking on the water towards the Lord, so long as we keep our eyes fixed confidently on him and put our lives in his hands.

IX

LEARNING TO SENSE THINGS

They have no wine left.—
Mary to Jesus (John 2. 3).

E. HELLO once said that "the glory of charity lies in sensing things". To sense distress which does not reveal itself, a mute appeal, a need which is not put into words, is one of the finest forms of human delicacy and charity.

Cana

Let us return once more to the scene, in the Gospel, of the marriage at Cana. The apostles, no doubt on the spur of the moment, went with their Master. The marriage feast was far from being over, and the supply of wine had almost run out. Mary noticed the embarrassment of a servant. She had sensed the family's uneasiness, and her plea came just before the moment when the shortage would have become noticeable. She turned to Jesus and spoke these simple words: "They have no wine left." She followed her intuition and acted on it. The miracle followed.

It is a characteristic of mothers to sense a mute supplication in a child's eyes, to see what passes unnoticed by others. A Christian, like a mother, should always be on the look-out and use his imagination.

For it needs imagination to put yourself in the place of another and look at things from somebody else's point of view. There are some people who seem to have been walled up alive. They are only interested in their own affairs. They are psychologically impervious to outside influences, like a stronghold without a drawbridge.

Comparing notes

How many homes are sad and desolate, simply because the wife is wrapped up in her household tasks and the husband in the private world of his professional work. Two lives are lived side by side, touching each other at every turn, without really affecting each other; not a glance of affectionate interest is cast from either side; each life is lived without reference to the other, and all the joy of it is lost. They are like two trains running on different lines. They seem to be heading in the same direction, but in fact they are always parallel and will never meet.

We can all make those around us happy. All we need is a little creative imagination. All we need to do is to change our position and look on the same scene, not from our own point of view, but from somebody else's.

Then, perhaps, the husband will realize that there is a lot of washing-up to be done, and it would be such a help if he lent a hand. The wife will feel an urge to take an interest in her husband's favourite sport and talk to him about it. The big boy will notice his little sister needs a playmate, and his big sister will remember that grandma has nothing to read or that her fire is not giving off enough heat. We must all put ourselves, in imagination, "on the other side".

Parents, you ought to sense what goes on in the minds of your children. The more they grow up, the more difficult this becomes, especially at the age when they want to assert their independence and establish a personality of their own while they are still in search of it. You ought to perceive intuitively the tremendous need of affection and sympathy which lies hidden behind their wildness, rudeness and contrariness. You ought to understand that an appeal may lie hidden beneath a refusal, that "no" may perhaps mean "yes", that an urge for something better is sometimes camouflaged by a layer of self-conscious scepticism or irony.

Children, you ought to sense what goes on in the minds of your parents and learn that their hearts remain very close to you, even if life separates you from them. You ought to sense their sadness if you are forgetful, or if you speak too sharply; sense the joy you can give by a letter, a telephone call or some mark of attention.

Understanding old people

We must try and understand the psychology of the old. After one of these family talks on the radio I got a letter from an elderly, unknown, but very appealing mother which made clear to me the sadness of growing old. Here are a few lines of it to help those who are still young to understand those who live side by side with them, but live in the past:

God, infinitely good as he is, knows and understands all our misery, our sense of loss, and above all our most distressing secret troubles. We cannot weep in front of those around us: they would not understand. They would say: "Why are you crying? You have all you need." No, in their eyes, you lack for nothing. But what our old hearts want is a warm ray of affection, a smile, especially those who miss the joy of feeling the little arms of a child round their neck from time to time. For when there are only grown-ups around, and they are always busy with their work and their worries, they've no time for us! And if at any time we try and take part in a conversation, we are quickly told that one cannot live today with the ideas of twenty-five years ago. Times have changed! We must be up to date— and we are at the end of our life's journey. Since, alas, we are not up to date, we must hold our tongues. We close our eyes to keep back our tears. Then it is that our inner tears fall like lead on our hearts. Who can understand that, unless he has suffered it himself? All we can do is doze at night in our lonely rooms, alone with old photographs and our old souvenirs which no one else wants, but which to us are relics. You can understand what a little it takes to hurt us and what a little to do us good. If our material needs are provided for, that is not enough: we also need tonics for our hearts and souls.

Understanding the poor

If we are rich, we must try to understand what goes on in the minds of the poor. To understand the psychology of the destitute, those who have nothing, you must forget your own comfort, look at things with their eyes, try to understand what it means to be almost dying of hunger, having to count your pennies, having to hide cleverly the fact that your suit is in pawn, and having to make one excuse after another for refusing an invitation which will cost you too much to accept.

Understanding the foreigner, the invalid

There are many other needs which we must also learn to understand.

What goes on in the mind of the refugee, the foreigner with no real home wandering in his country of exile? Thousands and thousands of men and women are still in this position. Let us pay attention to this kind of loneliness. Don't let us give anybody the impression that he is a nuisance, that he is out of place, or not wanted. It is a fine thing to make a gesture of fraternal welcome, and not make it look like a gesture of condescension.

You who are in good health, you should try to understand those who are not, and not weary them with pointless and idle conversation. Suffering, if it is accepted with a good heart, makes them develop, and opens up new horizons for them, leads them to hope for better things. They look to us for something more than trite and shallow utterances. They expect us to be able to listen to their silence and say the word which will cast a ray of bright, warm sunshine into their hearts and lives. They expect us to need them, need their prayers and sufferings to "pay off the debt which the afflictions of Christ leave still to be paid" (Col. 1. 24), so that the effects of the redemption can be felt in full.

Understanding the unbeliever

We who believe in God must learn to understand the man who does not. He does not blame us, mark you, for being Christians; he only blames us for not being Christian enough.

It is not unusual to hear people say: "You are lucky to believe in God. I envy you." And we ought to feel behind these words an appeal to be a faithful witness, an exhortation to make our witness plain to the eyes of our contemporaries.

In one of Claudel's plays, a little blind girl exclaims: "You people who can see, what do you do with the light?" This heart-rending appeal goes up to each of us who enjoy, without cost and without any merit on our part, the light of faith. Here again we must understand and respond, believe and speak, believe and hold out our hand humbly with a fraternal gesture.

I might go on indefinitely, but I must finish now. Let us all look around us with new eyes. A whole world of discovery will open up before us.

X

LEARNING TO TRUST

We have learned to recognize the love
God has in our regard, to recognize
it, and to make it our belief.— 1 John 4. 16.

EDUCATIONALISTS are always telling us that the secret of education is confidence in the person you want to educate. Nothing makes a child develop faster than confidence; nothing upsets him more than knowing he is not trusted. To trust is to run risks, but they are risks worth running.

The system of education in our schools is far from being a system of trust. Talking about a thing does not make it exist. We are too easily satisfied in this field.

Training in confidence ought to be undertaken seriously. What is true in human education is equally true in religious education. We must teach man to trust God. Our Lord was particularly insistent on this point. We certainly admire St Peter when he walks on the water. That seems to us a magnificent gesture of self-abandonment and courage. Now see St Peter stumble. Our Lord comes to his rescue, and what does he say to him?: "Why didst thou hesitate, man of little faith?" What God wants us to do is to give him our absolute trust, keep our eyes fixed on him. But we, we want to rely on ourselves; we want to take out guarantees, insurances. We find it so difficult to hand over the control of our lives to God.

Confident prayer

We find it so difficult to pray with confidence. For too many Christians, prayer is an insistent pleading to God to do our will, an announcement of what needs doing, and doing quickly, for what we think is our good. There is not an ounce of confidence in all this, but there is a good deal of anxious self-sufficiency. There is no need to petition God for our happiness, for that is something he never ceases to want. It is we who put obstacles in his way and hold his love in check. God always hears man's prayers, and God himself is the eternal answer. It is man who, too often, refuses to answer God.

So there is no need to ask ourselves whether all prayers are answered. They are answered the moment they become real prayers and to the extent that they are prayers, since they are really nothing more than the opening of the heart to the sacred entrance of the divine Presence. It is all summed up in the supreme appeal of the Apocalypse: "Come, Lord Jesus."

Praying with confidence does not mean praying with the conviction that God is going to do all I ask. It means praying with certainty that God is going to answer me as God knows how to, that is, like a Father who is infinitely loving, who knows everything, sees everything and who will give me the best of answers. But this answer may disappoint my expectation and be the exact opposite of what I want. God loves us infinitely more than we love ourselves. To trust is to believe in the overwhelming love of God; just as firmly when he goes against our wishes as when he seems to walk in step with us and fall in with our views. Trusting means closing our eyes and leaving everything to him. There are so many prayers which are just expressions of impatience and selfishness. They lack the serenity of the child who knows he is loved and in safe hands.

"I can see you and that's all that matters: jump"

This is a news item which was reported in the papers. A fire started one night in a house. The moment the flames broke out, the mother, father and children came rushing out and stood gazing in despair at the sight of their house on fire. Suddenly they noticed that the youngest child, a little boy of five, was missing. He had been frightened by the smoke and flames, and just as they were leaving the house he had turned back and had run upstairs again. They all looked at each other. There was no possibility of venturing into what was already beginning to be a blazing furnace. Then a window opened upstairs. The child was calling for help.

His father saw him and called out to him: "Jump." The child could see nothing but the smoke and the flames, but he heard his father's voice and answered: "Daddy, I can't see you." "But I can see you," his father called back, "and that's all that matters: jump!" And the little boy jumped. He was caught as he fell, and found himself safe and sound in his father's arms.

Is not this child, standing by himself at the window of a house on fire, an image of the Christian before God? He, too, hears in his distress the voice of God saying to him: "Trust me, jump into my arms."

To anyone who prays badly due to lack of confidence I would like to say in a similar way: "God can see you; that's all that matters; jump."

And I venture to add that when you do jump, when you make, that is, an act of confidence in God, you will by that gesture of self-abandonment be saying the most beautiful of prayers, the prayer God always answers by throwing his arms wide open.

"But I can see you; that's all that matters: jump."

We ought to let these words sink deep into our souls. There is no need for us to see; we must not expect the beatific vision in advance. On earth we are walking in the dark. God sees us, that's the thing that matters. He never leaves us at any time. He is holding us by the hand, even if we cannot feel him. God sees us. God knows. That is all we need to make us jump into his arms.

Ask the Blessed Virgin for the grace of filial confidence.

Mary walked in the darkness, knowing nothing, seeing nothing. But she said "yes" like a child, and God worked miracles of grace in her.

What we must do is go to her school, the school of absolute trust. And God will know how to answer us, far more than we hoped or desired, by opening to us here on earth the kingdom of those things "no eye has seen, no ear has heard, no human heart conceived," but which "God has prepared for those who love him" (1 Cor. 2.9).

XI

LEARNING TO FEEL FOR OTHERS

Who is weak, and I am not weak?—
St Paul (2 Cor. 11. 29).[1]

WE are living at one of the saddest moments of our country's history.[2] Our eyes and hearts are turned to that colliery at Bois du Cazier, Marcinelle, where the fate of two hundred and sixty-one men, a hundred and seventy of them fathers of families, hangs in the balance. The latest news is that the situation remains tragically uncertain, there is a curtain of fire in front of the main body of miners, holding them prisoner in the underground tunnels.

To realize how poignant this drama of the mine is, you have to see it on the spot: families with ravaged faces, exhausted by fatigue and long hours of anxious waiting; the grave and silent rescue-workers, who risk their lives and go down in relays with unself-conscious heroism.

This heart-rending spectacle calls forth the same spontaneous question from every heart: "What can we do to help?"

Material aid has poured in from all sides, in a

---

[1] Douay version.
[2] This talk was given at the time of the colliery disaster at Marcinelle, Belgium.

wonderful outburst of generosity, human solidarity and Christian charity. But there is room for spiritual aid to play its part with the same unanimous fervour.

These suffering men, women and children need to be enfolded in our prayers. Only prayer can penetrate to the deepest levels of the soul. Only prayer can descend to such depths, like the rescue-worker who drops down the shaft to bring relief. There are times when human speech sounds hollow, there are some wounds God alone can touch, because he is Light and Warmth, because his grace alone can pierce the hard shell of human grief and reveal the gleam of a hope that the world cannot give.

Condolence charged with hope

When prayer has created an atmosphere of peace and filial resignation to the will of God, there is still one duty to be done for those who suffer: we must explain to them, calmly, the meaning of the suffering which is crushing them. Who does not feel man's impotence at such moments, the emptiness of conventional sympathy and of words without reference to eternity, words without the hope of meeting again, the hope of resurrection? What can you say to a mother whose son's life has come to an end in the grave? What can you say to a wife, if human life itself is walled up in that earth, like those miners at the bottom of the pit, with no hope of escape, no way out to a world of light and peace? Do not forget that you carry Christ within you, and that he possesses the words of eternal life. Be Christ, be the Saviour, carry the words of life into these houses of mourning. You have no right to speak like those without hope. You have no right to be content with conventional sympathy and less still to use the empty words the pagans use. Go to those who are suffering. Let your way of speaking show that Christ is speaking through you. Even if it is only one word, let it be charged with light and hope.

The image of the Crucified

And if you cannot find a single word to say, or if grief makes all conversation impossible, then at least *do* something. Show them the crucifix. The image of the Crucified will speak instead of you and tell them the ultimate meaning, the redemptive value, of human suffering.

You have only to look at him there, incarnate Innocence, Justice and Love, you have only to contemplate, in his mangled flesh nailed to the cross, the marks of the passion he had done nothing to deserve, to understand that suffering is a mystery that is beyond us and that has its solution elsewhere.

There is a well-known passage of Claudel, pregnant with meaning: "Christ did not come to do away with suffering; he did not come to explain it; he came to fill it with his presence."

Weigh these words. "Christ did not come to do away with suffering," suffering born of man's own rebellion, engineered by the being whom Jesus called the Prince of Darkness. But Christ came to take it up, to wear it as a garment, or better still, to identify himself with it to the point of becoming the Man of Sorrows.

Christ did not come to explain suffering: he came to fill it with his presence, to fill it to the brim as we fill a goblet. To make it live with his presence, making a kind of sacrament of it, a palpable instrument of his grace at work. All suffering is a participation in the mystery of Good Friday. We must lift our eyes to Calvary if we want to try to perceive the meaning of redemptive suffering.

On the evening of Good Friday, darkness covered the earth, and the disciples questioned each other in anguish. Everything seemed to be over, and the women who came in tears next day to embalm the body had only one question on their lips: "Who is to roll away the stone for us from the door of the tomb?" (Mark 16. 3).

To the eyes of man it was midnight, and midnight marks the end. But to the eyes of faith, midnight brings in the dawn, midnight ends with Easter morning: life will spring up from the empty tomb. Since Christ emerged, alive, from the tomb, death has changed its meaning for us. The dead are no longer annihilated, but more alive than ever. The eyes that were closed are not closed for ever: they are open now to another light. The poet has put it better than anyone else could:

> Blue eyes and brown, beloved, bright,
> Lovely eyes that knew the dawning;

Now they sleep in the grave's dark night—
And the sun still rises every morning.

Blue eyes and brown, beloved, bright,
Open now to a glorious new dawning,
Beyond the gloom of the grave's dark night—
The eyes we closed still see the morning.

Let us make our way, then, to the families in mourning and speak to them calmly, as friends, about the resurrection of Christ. Perhaps they will not understand at first. Our patient and brotherly charity will help them to look up to heaven, the best of all meeting-places, the home which cannot be broken up, our Father's house where he is waiting for us all.

For if our dead have reached the end of their earthly course, we too are in sight of our own, and the suddenness of their death is a warning to us to be watchful.

"A Christian," said General de Sonis, "must always be prepared for two things: holy communion, and death." As a matter of fact, these two things are the same; for, to a Christian, to die is to receive communion, to be in communion with the love of God who stretches out his unseen arms to us, to be in communion with his joy, his beatitude, his peace.

It is good, in the darkness, to believe in the Light.
It is good, in the midst of tears, to believe in Joy.
It is good, in the midst of death, to believe in Life.

It is good to look death in the face with the eyes of hope; like the saint who, when she was dying, pointed to the wall of her cell and said: "Oh! death for me means to see this wall crumble away and to fall into the arms of God."

The wall crumbling away.... The arms of God, stretched out for the most wonderful of all embraces. ... This is the whole Christian meaning of suffering, ending in a mystery of peace.

XII

LEARNING TO READ

And Philip, as he ran up, heard him
reading the prophet Isaias, and asked,
Canst thou understand what thou art
reading? How could I, said he,
without someone to guide me?—Acts 8. 29-31.

KNOWING how to read: isn't that the easiest and
simplest thing on earth? No, not if learning to read
means learning how to react to what you read, knowing how to choose your reading and meditate on it.
It is not so simple or so widespread an accomplish-
ment as you might think.

Reacting to what you read means adopting a
critical, positive attitude, in which you examine and
judge what is before you.

Critical reading

Whether we like it or not, we are swamped by one
wave of printed matter after another, beginning with
the paper we read at breakfast. It is easy enough to
swallow it all, to be like soft wax on which the
printed characters impress themselves. After listening
for five minutes to the men sitting next to you in the
train, you can tell what kind of paper most of them
read. No, learning to read is not easy, when it means
not being taken in by the paper which is offered to us.

It is as well to be aware of the subtle power of

printed paper. The enormous changes which have taken place in public opinion during the last thirty years are the result of an appeal, not to the mind, but to the eye. In other words, public opinion no longer assesses the importance of events from the more or less persuasive arguments of a journalist, but from the layout and typographical setting of a paper. Two men reading the same news, the same telegram, in two different newspapers react in completely different ways, if one paper has splashed it under a banner headline and the other has inserted it under a nondescript heading.

Now this practically amounts to the complete "conditioning" of the reader; not the careful reader, of course, but the masses.

The Pope's appeal

You can see why Pope Pius XII, faced with the danger of a passive attitude in these matters, was able to say:

It is important that the critical sense of young people should be carefully formed by the time they are entering social and civic life; not, certainly, to flatter the taste for criticism to which that stage of life is only too prone, nor to encourage their spirit of independence, but rather to teach the young to live and think like men in a world where the means of diffusing news and ideas have acquired so compelling a power of persuasion. Learning how to read a newspaper, judge a film, criticize a performance, in a word, how to maintain control of one's judgment and feelings against everything which tends to depersonalize man, has become a necessity for us today.

What must we do to be on our guard? One way is, not to read just anything, but to make a judicious and thoughtful choice.

Knowing how to choose

In our reading, we are too often at the mercy of chance. The display of a book in a bookshop, a neighbour full of enthusiasm about the latest novel he has read, the snobbishness associated with having read the book everyone is talking about—all this causes us to open our minds to the most incongruous things. If your stomach had to put up with a diet of this kind, it would soon be out of order. You have to be selective about your food—and about your books. The influence they have on you is too great for you not to be clear and conscious of your responsibility for choosing them.

I will quote at random two passages which will hardly be suspected of dogmatism. One is from Jean Rostand and is to be found in a literary journal which opened its columns to men of science in very different fields, so that they could tell the world what their aspirations were. This is what he wrote: "Without doing anything to disturb what is sacred in liberty of expression, I wish we could find some way of

protecting French youth from the increasing poison-
ousness of certain literature."

The other quotation is from André Gide, who is just
as far from being a Christian: "I have read a certain
book, and, when I had read it, I put it back on a
bookshelf in my library. But in that book there was
an expression I cannot forget. It has penetrated me
so completely that I can no longer distinguish between
it and myself. From now on, I can no longer be as if
I had never known it. I may forget the book where I
read those words: I may even forget that I did read
them; I may only have an imperfect recollection of
them.... No matter! I can no longer be what I was
before."

Those are grave words. They are a warning to us,
as Christians, to take great care, as conscience dictates, about the choice of our reading. We have no
right to read anything we like on the pretext that it
has no effect on us. If we think we are immune, the
danger is that we may already have the virus in our
blood, and one day it will take its revenge. We cannot
replace our souls; we have no right to endanger the
honesty of our intelligence, the integrity of our faith,
the freshness and purity of our heart. You cannot play
about with these things with impunity.

We must be bold enough to pick and choose; we
must put a ban on reading which we feel to be harmful, even if the Index gives us permission to read it.

Wholesome reading

But perhaps this is all rather negative. We need

something positive as well to enrich our faith and improve our spiritual and religious culture. I would suggest that you devote some part of each day to reading of an inspiring, improving and sanctifying character. That is what is called, in ecclesiastical language, spiritual reading, meditative reading. Sometimes we need to fill our lungs with fresh air: experts in hygiene are very insistent about that. The Church calls for the same thing on the spiritual plane. In the rush and bustle of a busy day, we need a chance to stop for a while and be ourselves, in God's presence, with a book. A few lines read slowly, as a dialogue with the Saviour; better still, listening to him speak between the lines; what refreshment, what a tonic for the spiritual life!

What kind of book? The Gospels, first of all, obviously. They always have a message for us which comes straight from God. But there are other channels, streams and rivers from the same source, carrying the same waters into our land. From this store of invigorating reading, I would specially recommend to you the Lives of the Saints.

There was a time when these provided our fathers with food for thought in the long winter evenings. Now we have left them on one side. Their antiquated style often made the reading of them a penance. It is not so today. There are plenty of such lives now available which are excellent both in form and content. The saints have something to say to us. We should not ignore them, for they are God's great witnesses. If we need an antidote to the poisonous atmosphere we breathe, lives like these are worth their weight in gold.

The saints are Christians who have made a success of their lives. They are Christianity's heroes. Our way lies in the plain, but we shall find it stimulating to lift our eyes occasionally to their heights. It will help us perhaps to feel a little less like outsiders when we meet them in paradise! Meanwhile, they do us the invaluable service of helping us to breathe fresh air and they act as a counterbalance to so much reading which threatens, if we do not resist, to corrupt our souls.

XIII

LEARNING TO SMILE

Your gladness will be one which nobody can take from you.—
Jesus to his apostles (John 16. 22).

FATHER LEBBE found a friend of his in low spirits one day, looking sad and worried, and said to him, jokingly: "My friend, you've lost your sense of humour. It is time you made a retreat." Joy is the test of Christian vitality in a nation and in an individual soul, and this sign, by which the disciple of Christ is known, ought to be seen on his face. Cardinal Mercier used to say that by the time a man reached forty he was responsible for what he looked like. To this I would add that a Christian should bear the sign of joy on his countenance.

The Gospel, a message of joy

When Jesus began to preach his good news—the meaning of the word "Gospel" is message of joy and gladness—he opened the Sermon on the Mount with a torrent of words, all of the same kind: "Blessed are the poor in spirit. . . . Blessed are the patient. . . . Blessed are the peace-makers. . . . Blessed are those who mourn."

In Christian speech, there is a connection between the words "happy" and "blessed" and the very essence of the spiritual life. That does not mean that life should be without suffering or shock. No, joy and sorrow co-exist in the Christian life, but not on the same level; rather like the new capital of Brazil, where there are no traffic problems, because the streets cross at different levels. Suffering does not destroy hope; joy lies at a depth beyond the reach of man. Joy is something Christ himself expressly promised to his disciples: "Your gladness will be one nobody can take from you." The promise was explicit, the pledge sacred. And Jesus emphasized his statement when he said: "For my yoke is easy, and my burden light." In spite of the apparent contradiction we find in some tragic situation or other, there is nothing misleading about these words.

But the eyes of faith are needed to pierce the darkness. It is hard to believe in the sun when the clouds hang low and threatening, yet the sun is always there, faithful and true.

What a source of peace and joy for those who are suffering! For the Master's statement, "my yoke is easy, and my burden light," prevails in spite of all appearances to the contrary, and remains true for all times and all places. Nothing can happen to gainsay these words: they dominate facts, they overcome them, they create them. They will be proved true, even if a miracle is needed to do so. But there is one condition: like the Blessed Virgin at the time of the Annunciation, when she summed up her complete obedience to the will of God in this one phrase: "Let it be done to me according to thy word," we must offer no resistance. Right to the very core of her being, Mary had been fashioned by the Word: all her submission to God's will cries out in the joy of her *Magnificat*.

Every Christian who is obedient to the law of God holds the key of serenity and joy in his hands, if he submits in a filial way to all the demands of that law. Christianity is in itself a source of happiness to the individual, the family and society.

The school of the saints

The lives of the saints are a splendid illustration of the fact that Christianity is the source of joy. Their outlook on the world is bright and luminous, full of sunshine, leaving no room for doubt about the inner fire which consumes them. The greatest of their gifts was their smile. Let us imitate them; it is the very least we can do for others. Even if we have nothing to give, even if we cannot give them a helping hand, we can make their path through life brighter with a smile. To smile is to look at others with the eyes of Christ. A smile is a luminous ray from the face of God. When you smile at a stranger, you are telling him that you recognize him and accept him as a brother.

I have always been struck by these words of St Thérèse on the subject of heaven: "In heaven, there will be no more looks of indifference." What a contrast heaven will be to this world, with all the crowds of people we meet with their averted gazes and hard and indifferent faces. Let us be sowers of joy. A smile creates bonds between men, creates bridges between them, makes friends. In other words, it turns the human community into one great family and, if only for a second, takes people out of their cold and hostile anonymity.

A smile is a foretaste of paradise. It is like the reflection of another world. Some smiles are signs of victory. Is there anyone who does not cherish the memory of some invalid, some person at the point of death, whose smile of joy was a triumph of courage and resignation in affliction? Think of the smile of St Bernadette, which her contemporaries all found so striking, which came to her straight from the smile of Our Lady herself, who had marked her for ever with her imprint.

To smile is to forget yourself for the sake of others, to let God shine through you. Men know that well enough: that is why they smile instinctively when they bend over a child's cradle: one of the loveliest sights this world has to show, which comes straight from heaven.

One smiles spontaneously at children, sensing their freshness, their naturalness, their innocence.

When a person smiles at other people he brings out all that is best in them; he does more: he brings the child in the grown man to life again, liberating his real self from the hard shell of conformity, freeing his liberty from all restraint. It is such a good thing to do!

A touch of humour—a smile in another form—is a form of good will which can relieve tension in difficult situations and put many things into perspective. It is like a breath of fresh air in a stuffy room: we breathe more freely. There is a lot of self-forgetfulness in the kind of humour which puts things in their proper proportion. If laughter, as Bergson says, is born of contrast, of the unexpected in a situation, the Christian, who by definition has the sense of the absolute, should also have a better sense of the relative than others and avoid over-dramatizing things. Men are generally better, at heart, than they seem, and they appreciate being treated accordingly.

A smile is an invitation addressed to the real self, the self God sees when he looks down on the earth, the self we hope to be judged by. A smile is an invitation to a state of grace; it emerges like a flower from its stem. To know how to love men and smile at them, through our tears if need be, is to breathe in advance the atmosphere of heaven, where brotherly love, with nothing to mar its perfection, will hold sway in the one embrace which goes on for ever and starts with God himself.

XIV

LEARNING TO SHARE THINGS[1]

All the faithful held together,
and shared all they had.— Acts 2. 44.

Now we are in Advent, the season which leads us gradually to Christmas. What we all have to do now is to enter into the spirit of the first Advent, which, long ago, was lived through by the man and woman who, in the name of all of us, waited for the Christmas of Christmases. Mary and Joseph. Advent calls us to put ourselves at the feet of the Holy Family and ask them to help us by sanctifying our family life and making Christianity's chief blessing, joy, prevail within it. Advent offers us the grace of family renewal. I would like to dwell on this grace during the course of these talks and link it with your everyday problems as closely as possible. What better way is there of preparing for Christmas than making the family circle more welcoming, warmer and more brotherly?

Give and take in family life

I am going to talk to you this evening about one small duty of family life which is a wonderful help in creating that atmosphere of peace and joy: I want to talk about sharing, give and take in the family circle,

[1] The four talks which follow were given during the season of Advent and were meant as a preparation for Christmas.

putting into the common store the best that each member of the family has in him.

We all have the same longing deep down in our hearts to regard everyone else as a brother, one of the family, one of us. At first sight, human beings seem to be pursuing complicated and very different ends; they are engaged in business or politics, art or literature, ploughing the soil or sailing the seas. In reality, behind the façade of all these occupations, they are all searching for something extremely simple, something moving in its simplicity; they are in search of love. They are longing to love and be loved.

All men hunger and thirst for true love. They want a reason for living as fully as their hearts will let them.

I want to try to find out, in company with you, how best we can all help each other to find and experience in the home the mutual understanding, the intimate exchanges, the sharing of feeling and affection, which gives warmth and joy to the home.

We all know houses where all the members of the family live side by side as if they were in a boarding-house. They eat the same bread at the same table, but they live like strangers. Spiritually they are poles apart.

If you want to introduce a little warmth into surroundings like these, you will have to start by introducing a little warmth into your own heart, by sharing something more than bread—your heart and your life. We are all too wary about the intrusion of others, too fond of shutting ourselves up in our ivory tower; whether from timidity, shyness or resentment, I cannot say, but that's what happens. Men even manage to live in complete spiritual isolation, like hermits, when the best thing they could do to make life worth living, the greatest happiness they could give to those they live with would be to show them what they are really like.

When you get to know a person really intimately, it is always a surprise to find what an unknown world comes to light, what his outlook really is and generally how full of good will he is at heart.

Building bridges

How can we bridge the gap between men of good will? This is surely the question we have to face on the day before Christmas Eve, the great day for bringing people closer together. And if bridging gaps seems too much like hard work, let us make a start, at least, by putting down one or two little gangways, and by putting into practice those much-vaunted "human relations" the experts have been discovering in the field of economic or social productivity.

It is a problem as old as Christianity, but we can only rejoice at this discovery and all the work that is being put into it.

It is so much easier to be pleasant to passing strangers than to our own families: our families are not deceived by appearances. Why not try to establish good human relations at home first?

The temptation to self-sufficiency begins, if not at the moment of waking, at least with the reading of the morning paper. This is the first moment of the day when we are in danger of isolating ourselves. You know the familiar scene which takes place in one home after another! Father, engrossed in his newspaper, oblivious to his surroundings, wraps himself up in newsprint like a screen; and once he has consumed his daily ration of bread and news sets off, full speed, for the office.

If he emerged from his reading occasionally, if only to talk about some news item of the day, would that not be the first step towards good human relations? One word, a comment or two, and the gap has been bridged. The newspaper is no longer an insulator, no longer as hermetically sealed as a polling-booth, but a meeting-point, a common centre of interest. The children feel grown up and the wife understands that she exists for her husband on another plane than the domestic.

That is only one example and it will serve as a symbol. The day is full of such opportunities, and we must not fail to take advantage of them.

It will not be difficult for any of us to find out what we should share with others and what we should keep to ourselves. We should all keep the happiness of others in mind, and keep a daily look-out for the things which create and foster it.

A day in the family circle is like a mosaic composed of tiny little pieces which have to be placed next to each other to make up the whole. There is no beauty in a mosaic, unless each detail contributes to the over-all effect and unless each piece is in place. Love is built up stone by stone, each act is necessary for the harmony of the whole. Let us all ask ourselves this evening what we have contributed to the family circle. If the examination of conscience proves negative, let us offer the Lord our good will to do better tomorrow.

XV

LEARNING TO FORGET

> *I will not remember their sins*
> *and their transgressions any more.—*
> St Paul (Hebrews 10. 17).

Forgiving injuries

IT is most important to learn how to forget. That may sound paradoxical if what we forget are the things of the mind which we have accumulated by reading, study and what is called general culture. Hasn't culture been defined by somebody as "what you have left when you've forgotten everything you learnt"? There is a disencumbering of the brain, a cutting out of dead matter, which gives new life and strength: are not trees pruned in readiness for the Spring?

But this is not the kind of forgetfulness I am talking about now. If we intend to live the Christian life as our Saviour has defined it, we must learn to forget things which belong to the realm of the soul, particularly the injustices we have suffered. The words of the Gospel cannot be slurred over for fear that they should offend our susceptibilities. Now, the Gospel speaks about forgiving injuries in terms which are only too clear; we cannot pretend we do not understand them. Besides, one of the petitions of the Our Father pulls us up sharp. When the disciples asked the Master to teach them how to pray, Jesus ended his model prayer with these words: "Forgive us our trespasses as we forgive them that trespass against us." In other words: "Forget as we forget." Do you notice the parallel? We ask God to treat us as we treat others. That is, so to speak, burning our boats. After that, if we do not forgive, how can we expect God to forgive us?

The temptation of Pharisaism

This makes little impression on us, it is true, since we are scarcely aware of having any faults to forgive. We need to undergo a course of re-education: we are too satisfied with ourselves, too perfect in our own eyes.

This is a subtle and persistent temptation. Jesus has already put us on our guard against Pharisaism, that disease good people suffer from. The saints know better than anyone how to forgive injuries, because they know they are sinners themselves. This is no paradox. When St Francis said he was the greatest sinner in the world, he believed it; he knew better than anyone the flagrant disproportion between the graces he had received and the way he had responded to them. The saints are so conscious of being sinners that their consciences are not sullied by any temptation to self-satisfaction.

That is the way the saints regard themselves.

Whether we are convinced that we are sinners or not, the Master's command is explicit: we must forgive as God forgives us. Here again we are very good at indulging in a clear piece of casuistry. How often we hear the phrase—and it is certainly a sign of progress, a step forward—"I forgive, but I do not forget." A futile piece of subtlety: to forgive is precisely to forget; to efface and start again. God's forgiveness even goes as far as wiping out the fault, but that is a privilege reserved to God alone. What we do is stick the broken pieces of a vase together. God makes it all over again in one piece.

However imperfect our human forgiveness is, we still have to forget the past as best we can, and take the first step towards the one who has wounded and offended us. Take two men who have quarrelled over money, or an insult; take a husband and wife between whom there is coldness. Words have been said, bitter words, which they have thought better of, but they cannot bring themselves to admit it openly. Each is hypnotized by the real or imaginary wrong the other has done. What should the Christian do?

The first step

By way of parenthesis, let me tell you about a question which, it seems, was once put to a marshal of France. Two generals were at loggerheads over a question of precedence. Which of them should salute first? They were equal in seniority, both the same age, both the same rank. The marshal gave his answer: "The one who is most polite."

Coming back to the quarrel I was talking about, let me ask my question: "Who is to take the first step, make the first gesture, the first effort at reconciliation?"

The one who is most Christian.

Sometimes, unfortunately, it is not just a temporary upset; discord even unfaithfulness, has reared its ugly head in the family circle. Elsewhere,[1] I have tried to explain what the demands of the law of forgiveness are in conjugal matters.

The innocent partner must love more than ever, not merely with human love, but with Christian love, a love which has been raised to a higher plane, enriched with God's own love.

In such cases, what is required of the truly Christian partner is to love the other infinitely more and infinitely better, not merely with his poor, wounded, human love, but with the love of God.

Our short lived human wisdom finds it hard to take on the outlook of this magnanimous love, this supreme demand of Christianity. The faithful partner must love with the very heart of God; and that means, with love whose qualities are not of this world.

God loved man first, as John expressed it in an unforgettable phrase. His love is a free gift; it does not depend on our response. It does not waver if we betray him. God's love is unrelenting and disinterested. He loves us in spite of our impurity and unfaithfulness. He is subject to no vexations which drive him into his shell, no susceptibilities which can be aroused or wounded. The faithful partner, if he wants to live up to what God expects of him at such times, if he wants, so far as it depends on him, to save his home, must make his own this great, persevering and unwearying love.

[1] See *Love and Control*, pp. 85-86.

Who does not know those poignant cases where unfaithfulness, open or concealed, is present? What can be done in the face of such distress? Humanly speaking, nothing. From the Christian point of view, we must read once again those passages in the Gospel in which Jesus commands us to forgive up to seventy times seven, even at the risk of being slighted and made a fool of again, at the risk of encountering concealed ingratitude and contempt.

When all efforts at saving the marriage have proved vain, we must have the courage to go on loving and wait patiently, not take refuge in recriminations and reproaches, but love like the father of the prodigal son, who waited for the return of the penitent sinner with a love stronger and greater than sin. This unfaithful man or woman is still the person entrusted by God to the faithful partner, even if the union can never again be realized in this world.

The Christian is forbidden to take refuge in divorce; that would be another act of betrayal. A mother loves her son, whatever he does; a mother does not divorce her son. To his wife, the unfaithful husband is still, before God, her first child. She must still love him, as one loves an invalid, and, in the secret places of her heart, guard the treasure God has irrevocably entrusted to her.

These are hard and heroic words. God offers an abyss of suffering to the man or woman who undergoes the ordeal of infidelity. But that is the way of the Gospel. There is no other way but this which leads, through tears, to peace and joy. This is the peace "which nobody can take away from you", the peace our Lord has promised to one who serves him to the end. At the hour of death, he will have the joy of knowing how love like his avails for the redemption of the one who betrayed love.

Self-forgetfulness

But it is not only in the home that discord causes trouble. It threatens at every step the understanding between men of good will. There is a temptation to identify our self-esteem with the work we are doing and to refuse to pardon on the grounds that principles are threatened or authority itself called in question. Let us beware of such subtlety, and open the Gospels with humility: on every page we learn that mercy and forgiveness come before anything else.

XVI

LEARNING TO GIVE
ENCOURAGEMENT

*All this I have told you, so that my
joy may be yours, and the measure of
your joy may be filled up.—*
Jesus to his apostles (John 15. 11).

I WANT to talk to you about a human and Christian
duty that is little known and, in general, badly practised: the duty of giving encouragement. We are so
apt to forget that criticism, if it is to do any good, must
be constructive; it must be part of a common effort
for improvement and spur us on to do better.

Take care that criticism does not develop into an
obsession. It is a harmful habit. Few can resist the
corrosive effect of criticism, few have courage, enthusiasm and humour enough to go ahead in spite of
disapproval.

The need for encouragement

Men need their normal quota of encouragement.
They need, occasionally at least, a few rays of sunshine. Look at the wonderful results you can get by
encouraging a child when he deserves it. Look at the
harm you do if you behave in the opposite way. You
have only to travel by train or tram to see examples
of how not to bring children up. A little child
has just played some prank or other: a torrent of

threats begins to descend on his head, and, incident-
ally, these threats are often not really meant to be
taken seriously and the child himself does not do so:
don't make any mistake about that.

Parents who know how to get obedience from little
boys of three or four, who, even at that age, are trying
out their independence, are few and far between. So
what we see is a test of endurance. The child feels
that with a little obstinacy on his part, and a flood of
tears if need be, he will have the last word. Generally
the parents give in for the sake of peace: defeated,
they take refuge in impotent recriminations.

It would be much better to stick to a settled order of
things, and then assist weak and young wills with
suitable encouragement. I do not say encourage by
promising them something which would spoil them,
but by a word which will help them to do better, by
emphasizing the good efforts they have made and by
showing that something better is expected from them.
How many children would have done infinitely
better at school and at home if teachers and parents
had been less parsimonious with praise and approval.

Yet it only takes a minute to say the word that brings
out latent energy, and spurs on to greater efforts.
This is true of any kind of training, even for the
simplest things. How did we learn to ride a bicycle?
Wasn't it because somebody lifted us into the saddle,
held us up, told us again and again not to worry about
trees, all we had to do was look straight in front of us,
everything was all right, we were nearly there, we
were there.

What is true in child-training is true for adults throughout life; very often they still have the hearts of children, and are too shy and awkward to make overtures. We must not overlook the fact that shyness is a very common state, and a rather attractive one at that, so long as it does not prevent enthusiasm or make people withdraw into themselves. We ought to realize that, all around us, there are men and women who, because they are shy, live withdrawn into themselves, like the petals of a flower before the sun comes up. We all know that the sun makes flowers open, while cold and darkness make them close up. A word of encouragement has a magical effect on people: it brings them out and cheers them.

Opportunities to seize

We are too miserly with our encouragement. Everyone should examine his conscience on this matter. Husbands, do you give any encouragement to your wives while they are slaving away on behalf of you and the children? When I say "encouragement" I don't mean just a word of thanks, but a special gesture of appreciation when they have gone to some extra trouble or done something on their own initiative. So many people take it all for granted. They only think of what their near and dear ones owe them: they never think of their own obligations. Wives, do you ever think of encouraging your husband in his job, in his efforts at self-improvement, his devotion to the apostolate, even if that deprives you of his company at the fireside on occasion? Does it never occur to you that, after the pinpricks and the boredom of work at the office, he feels some sort of need to escape, a desire to get back to that atmosphere of buoyancy at home which comes of the trust his family show in him?

What is true in the family circle is equally true in all forms of social life. Masters and servants, employers and employees, chiefs and subordinates, we all need to examine our consciences.

What men want from each other is not money, but something quite different. They want people to stop when they meet, take notice of them, be aware of their existence and show it from time to time. Nothing is more encouraging than to find people ready to take notice of you, to show a real regard for you and to give you encouragement when you least expect it, so long as it all comes naturally and is not the forced courtesy of some social occasion.

We ought to look at the people around us, the people we think of too often as part of the framework of our existence, rather like an armchair, a clock or a cupboard, and put ourselves in their place.

We must fully realize this: the people around us are not just pieces of machinery or furniture. They like us to be aware of their existence, they like to be noticed occasionally. Encouragement is one of the many aspects of active charity. For this reason we ought to take every opportunity of giving publicity to the good that is done throughout the world. We are served up with column after column of news about crimes, thefts, Khrushchev's invective, assassinations, to say nothing of attempted suicides. It would be pleasant to find at least one column (one of the weeklies actually has one) devoted to the outstanding good deed; to discover some quiet little corner, like an oasis in the desert, where prominence was given to secret devotion and brave deeds done by men who left without giving their names. The world would be a much better place if people knew how to encourage their neighbours to achieve the good they longed to do, if they knew how to say the right word at the right time, the word which galvanizes men into action and which improves them.

One of the forms Christian charity takes is the art of encouragement. It is an art which is in everybody's reach. All you have to do is to keep your eyes and ears open and have an open heart.

XVII

LEARNING TO RELAX

> *Come away into a quiet place by*
> *yourselves, and rest a little.—*
> Jesus to his apostles (Mark 6. 31).

Necessary relaxation

MODERN life is lived at high tension; nerves get frayed, the pace of life is intense. Whatever it costs, we must learn how to stop, when we need to, and draw a quiet breath. Men solve the problem of necessary recreation by taking more week-ends and holidays. That is a step forward. But we must still learn how to relax, how to avoid being unbalanced by amusements, how to measure out this rhythm of fatigue and repose, work and recreation, in the required mixture. It is most important that rest should be soothing and that recreation, as the word implies, should re-create, create us over again, give us new life, a fresh start. We are a long way from that: how many tourists do their touring on the piece-work system! They eat up the miles, they tear through the countryside, see nothing, and come back more exhausted than when they started. This applies not only to tourism, but to the cinema and TV, and it can even be true of reading if we fail to learn the art of relaxing in order to work better.

In order to acquire this art, we must learn particularly how to take advantage of the little opportunities life has to offer and become children at heart again.

We must not live at such an intensive, hustling pace that we no longer have time to ... have time. To be relaxed makes one accessible to others.

Relaxation in the home

Parents, ask yourself occasionally during the feverish activity of the day whether you are sufficiently approachable to your children, especially the older ones. It is so easy to get to the stage of being so caught up in our work that we never really have time to be with others. We rush about and get involved in business when we ought to be able to sit down and listen; even, when the atmosphere is intimate enough, to sit down in silence together. So many things need the right atmosphere, the slow and gradual approach.

Time has no respect, it has been said, for anything that is done without reference to time : time is needed to ripen a field of corn or make a flower come out. Our family life is too rushed. The home too often becomes a sort of boarding-house from which everyone sets off on his own affairs, a cross-roads where we pass each other. We no longer live together, breathe together, sing together, play together. Now all these things go a long way to promote unity of hearts and minds. We must try and preserve in our homes a modicum of recreation in common, something we can all do together, and find time for family prayer in the evening. What a blessing the family rosary is! Those *aves* link souls together more effectively than the rosary beads are linked! Prayer is a bond, a link, a union.

Happy the home where husband and wife read the same book and compare notes afterwards; where everyone shares, not just the bread which perishes, but the interests, the joys and the sorrows of others. We are too apt to think that amusements must be expensive if they are to be appreciated. How often the child of the rich is sad and miserable with his luxurious toys; how often the children of the poor are as happy as sandboys with their whips and peg-tops! The key of happiness is within us; joy can only be measured by our own hearts.

The Master's example

We must learn, or re-learn, to have time. Our Lord himself did not want his apostles to live in a state of perpetual tension. He urged them to "come away into a quiet place": "rest a little," he said to them one day after they had finished their apostolic missions. In the wilderness and in solitude, he revealed to them the best of himself and his message. Our Lord paid a great deal of attention to time and the gradual approach. How often he said to his apostles: "It is not for thee to know, now, what I am doing; but thou wilt understand it afterwards," or "My time has not yet come," "The time is coming. . . ."

The duty of sitting down

We stand in need of rest; rest in the ordinary sense of the word, and also rest in God. We must find a place for him in the bustle of the day; a place for private prayer, for slow and meditative reading. We need this "oxygen". No luxury this; it is one of our vital necessities. It is a good thing to sit down, like Mary, at the feet of the Master before we go off to carry out our indispensable daily tasks. In the midst of work, we must keep our hearts open to God. It helps so much to keep things in their proper proportion if we keep a window open to heaven.

We must call a halt from time to time, and it is better to do it sooner than later. The Christian ought to take the trouble to find sound and wholesome forms of amusement. It is his job to christianize the vast world of entertainment. There is a Christian way of going out for the day and a Christian way of dancing. There is a way of life which it is our business to promulgate and ways of life we have no right to accept or tolerate. Christian parents, do not jeopardize the souls of your children by letting them go on "blind dates" where the moral atmosphere is beyond your control. Do not yield to the pressure of the young when they want to see everything and read everything in order to be up to date.

The more technological progress advances, the farther the vast field of leisure will stretch. Here is tremendous scope for Christian influence. In the past we have sinned by our negative attitude; we have too often been content to condemn without any attempt at participation on our part. We ought to be alive to this world in the making, where the way of life of the younger generation is in the balance. Don't blame the young, but learn how to find healthy and wholesome forms of amusement for them which respect their souls, their faith and their hearts. In all the capitals of the world there are complaints about the behaviour of the beatniks. The youth of today, for a variety of reasons, lack inner harmony, and so they try and forget their troubles by behaving badly or foolishly.

Sunday rest

We need to get our breath back. That is why the Church is so insistent on Sunday being kept as a holy day; a day for public worship, certainly, but also a day of rest. Don't let us make it the most hectic day of the week. Sunday should be distinguished from other days by rest, which is akin to recollection, rest which is not empty, but full to the brim. When, on a Sunday, we deck ourselves out in our best clothes, we should also, on this of all days, give ourselves a new heart, or at least a renewed heart. We must detach ourselves from our work, but only in order to attach ourselves more firmly to the one thing needful. We must stop, like the Alpine climber who has reached a high peak, to take breath for a moment, admire the view, fill our lungs with fresh air and go on to the next peak. Sunday is the day to halt so that we can resume our march with a firmer tread. Do not let us neglect to fix our gaze on the sky until we can see the stars shining there. We make much better headway here on earth when we have a sense of direction and move forward with a firm step on solid ground. Looking at the heavens is the form of relaxation we can least dispense with if we want to keep things in their perspective and make the world a better place to live in

XVIII

LEARNING TO LOVE LIKE A HUMAN BEING

*These are the directions I give you,
that you should love one another.*
—Jesus to his apostles (John 15. 17).

I want to talk about charity as a revolutionary force.

Charity gets a very bad press, as we all know, from the extreme right to the extreme left of contemporary thought.

Charity, a manly virtue

On the extreme right, how can we help remembering what was said about it by the racialist movement and its prophet Rosenberg, of evil memory? Charity, he told us, came from the East and was unworthy of man. A hothouse plant incapable of being transplanted in our northern climate, it was the fruit of eastern flabbiness and fear of living. It was effeminate, humiliating and degrading; it was abdication, treason and cowardice.

Its influence on Christianity, he explained, had to be eliminated. Christ himself was unacceptable, except as a strong man. The Christ who drove the money-changers out of the Temple could be accepted, but not the Master who proclaimed the beatitudes and died on the cross while praying for his executioners.

Is there any need to answer this? Nothing could be more artificial than this contrast, and Christianity as a whole protests against such a distinction. I am speaking, of course, of authentic Christianity, for attempts are occasionally made to acclimatize the most extreme pacifism in Catholic soil. They try to introduce a sentimental, miserable and non-human form of charity under the banner of evangelical charity. They quote one of the sayings of Jesus, torn from its context: "If a man strikes thee on the cheek, offer him the other cheek too; if a man would take away thy cloak, do not grudge him thy coat along with it. Give to every man who asks, and if a man takes what is thine, do not ask him to restore it" (Luke 6. 29-30).

Does Christian perfection, then, demand non-resistance to brutality, even in defence of the right? Must we renounce any form of self-defence?

No! You have only to read the Scriptures right through to see how Jesus himself and his disciples interpreted that command.

When the high priest's steward struck our Lord, he did not turn the other cheek, but said to him: "If there was harm in what I said, tell us what was harmful in it; if not, why dost thou strike me?" (John 18. 22).

Later on, it was St Paul's turn to stand his trial before the tribunal of Ananias. The high priest bade one of his guards smite the apostle on the mouth. Paul said to him:

"It is God that will smite thee, for the whitened wall thou art; thou art sitting there to judge me according to the law, and wilt thou break the law by ordering them to smite me?" (Acts 23. 3).

Will it be claimed that Paul failed to understand the Gospel or that Christ contradicted his own teaching?

No; the lesson Jesus was teaching in this passage was that we should not make a great deal of fuss about our rights, our personal, transferable rights. That has no bearing on the sacred rights entrusted to us, which we have to defend.

Charity has nothing in common with soft holy pictures or a sickly piety. Energy and vigour are its very foundations. It is a strong and manly virtue.

This is the one and only kind of charity I am going to talk about.

Charity, the complete virtue

Charity has also had to run the gauntlet of criticism at the other end of the scale, on the extreme left of contemporary thought. In the first place, it gets confused with almsgiving. But it is not that. Christian charity, and that is what I am to talk about, cannot be identified in any way with almsgiving, which has a dignity of its own, according to its rank and position, but is only one of the many and varied forms charity assumes.

Almsgiving is one of its manifestations, the form it takes in certain special cases. But it nowhere near covers the immense field of theological charity. Very well, someone may say, charity is not almsgiving; but charity can so easily serve as an alibi for justice; and it is on justice, not charity, that we want to build human society.

If charity were an alibi for justice, I should most decidedly cast my vote for justice, rather than charity.

It is evident that man's rights must be respected if he is to be loved as a man. Human society must be founded on respect for human dignity, and this respect presupposes fraternal equality between children of the same father, as also a passionate quest for social progress and the betterment of the lot of the under-privileged classes. But that is not what we are talking about.

Justice and charity

There is no case for preferring justice to charity, and still less for preferring charity to justice. For Christian charity, and that is what I am talking about, is already at the very heart of human justice.

A French philosopher has defined charity in these admirable terms: "It is undivided attention to the existence of another."

Few people take this interest in the existence of others. Few really consider that their neighbours exist! But if that is what charity is, it also includes, at its first step, on the rudimentary level, the interest I take in my neighbour when I respect his rights. The virtue of justice (I do not say the instinct) comes in the first place from love. It is the form love takes when it aims at restoring the original equilibrium between men and making an initial re-allocation of mine and thine; when it defines the minimum everyone can insist on if society is to be made to work.

But it is clear that a society ruled exclusively by justice would be like a barracks. Think of society as a group of passengers in a train or bus. There you have the reign of justice to perfection. Each man has paid for his seat, each has the equivalent of the "minimum living wage", except at the rush hour. Each is the equal of his neighbour and can do what he likes within reason.

But you will agree with me that, as a society, there is nothing very attractive about it. Why is that?

Because there is no room for the exercise of that human fellowship which true charity establishes among men.

Pope Pius XI, in *Quadragesimo Anno,* wrote these words:

> To ensure that these social reforms are fully carried out, we must rely, first and foremost, on the law of charity, the bond of perfection. Certainly, the exercise of charity cannot be thought of as replacing the duties of justice when there is a refusal to perform these duties; but even if everyone on earth were to get everything he was entitled to, there would still be plenty of scope left for charity.

Justice alone, even when scrupulously practised, is incapable of removing the causes of social conflict. It does not, of itself, bring about the reconciliation of wills or the unity of hearts. If artificial distinctions between justice and charity are to be avoided, two things must be understood: justice is a stricter obligation than charity, but charity is the social virtue *par excellence*.

The obligation is stricter and more limited in the case of justice, not because it is more perfect, but rather because it guarantees the protection of a minimum of charitable relations as the necessary condition for eventual progress in love.

"Justice," said Frederick Ozanam, "presupposes a large measure of love. We have to love men a great deal before we can respect their rights, if those rights restrict our own liberty." All contradictions disappear once you grasp the social dimension of charity emphasized by the Bishop of Tournai when he wrote: "What does it mean to love your neighbour as yourself? It is not just giving alms or showing benevolence towards individuals; it is something more: taking society itself under your wing to reduce its inequalities and make it resplendent with justice. It must not be forgotten that social progress can wipe out or alleviate the material and moral misery of millions of human beings at a single stroke."

This is the true face of Christian charity.

XIX

LEARNING TO LOVE LIKE GOD

God is love.—1 John 4. 16.

CHARITY, which I have placed mid-way between the two extremes which detract from its real nature, bears within itself an amazing revolutionary power.

If you want to see this in real life, all you need do is analyse the human heart left to its own natural powers, its own spontaneous impulses.

The weakness of the human heart

Whom do we really love?

It is easy enough to say that we love the whole of the human race; but we have to admit that the love we feel for the inhabitants of the North Pole is not the kind to make our hearts beat wildly.

Now the question is just this : how far do our human heart-beats go? Whom do we love naturally? Our near and dear ones, our relations, or friends and neighbours. I say neighbours in case we live in the country : if we live in town, we don't even know their names. Count them up for yourself and see what you make the total. Whatever it is, I think I can say that our capacity for loving soon exhausts itself.

And this is precisely the miracle that supernatural

charity works in us. It rushes into us like a torrent, breaks down our water-tight compartments and our Great Walls of China and quickly opens the heart to new dimensions, the very dimensions of the love of God. For charity is the love of God taking up its abode in the heart of a man, enlarging it, giving it an unexpected power and capacity. It is God who comes to love in us and wants to love through us. The more room we make for him, the more overwhelming it becomes.

There is an easy way to assess the effect of this revolution that God brings about within us, a test within the reach of everybody. Our Lord explains it in the Gospel, when he tells us to make a summary examination of conscience. Ask yourself, says Jesus, this question: "Will not the very heathen do as much?" (Matt. 5. 47). You pass the time of day with those who speak to you. Very good. Will not the very heathen do as much? You love those who love you. Very well. Will not the very heathen do as much? Then continue the review of your day on these lines until you find some deed you have done or some attitude of mind you have taken which cannot be explained in natural terms.

When you get to this stage, there is a good chance that you are on the right road and that the love of God is at work in you. If not, it's a good idea to ask yourself whether you are not deceiving yourself.

How often can we say: "What I have just done is something I should not have done without Christ"?

Think of the story of St Francis of Assisi travelling along the road on horseback. He comes across a leper who holds out his wooden bowl. Francis sees it, recoils with horror and, tossing him a purse full of crowns, takes to headlong flight. That is the natural reaction of the human heart. Now see this same Francis, impelled by God, stop his horse, turn back in his tracks, jump to the ground, go up to the leper and embrace him like a brother. That is not natural. A revolution has taken place in Francis's heart. The love of God has entered it, and it is with God's heart that he has come to love this man. God does not demand the same heroic deeds from us all, but he does ask us to lend him our hearts so that he can love men through us.

The power of God's heart

To be quite honest, we do sometimes feel the desire to love men *for the love of God*. That is not enough, and there is a risk of its becoming very artificial. Our human hearts need to be sustained not merely by the love of God from without, but transfigured from within.

We must do more than that. We are called upon to love men, not merely for the love of God, but with the very love God loves them with.

What a world of difference that makes. It is worth the trouble of taking a closer look at it. For if this is the way of it, our love has to take on the very properties of God's own love.

Love which comes first

Now, how does God love? First, let it be said that his love comes first. It is always God who takes the initiative in loving; it is always God who says the first word. The initiative always comes from him. It is extremely important that we should realize this: the love of God comes first, meets us half-way, and needs no motivating force but the impulse of his own heart.

Remember these claims of God's when a quarrel starts at home. And understand that, for a Christian, the one in the wrong is the one who does not take the first step.

Let me continue the analysis. Why do we human beings love the people we love? Because, surely, we discover in them affinities of soul and qualities we like. But once those qualities fade, once those affinities waver, our love is in danger of growing cold or dying out altogether.

We know what Pascal had to say about it: "He no longer loves that girl he loved ten years ago. I well know she is not the same person; nor is he, either."

The love of God, on the other hand, does not depend on our reaction to it, nor on our response. God loves us, if I may so express it, relentlessly. If we loved men with the love of God, if we really entered into that love, we should love them first, we should love them last, we should love them faithfully, whatever their response. We should love them with a love which comes first, untiring love, magnanimous love.

Love with no return

Only God can love without asking something in return. When we love, we stand to gain something by it. The man who gives his life for his brother perfects himself in the very act of self-sacrifice. He is enriched, and his soul gains stature. God cannot be enriched, since he is the fullness of all things, supreme riches. God can only give himself for nothing. He had nothing to gain by creating the world. That act of love was, therefore, the most magnanimous, the most generous imaginable. Hence we can understand that the Scripture should make the Lord say: "one mind they shall have, and a new spirit shall fill their inmost being; gone the heart of stone, and a human heart theirs in place of it" (Ezechiel 11. 19). This new heart is the heart of God himself, brought in to take the place of our own and accomplish his revolution.

Once the love of God has entered into a soul and the soul accepts all the demands of that love, the power which is God's own love becomes a power of invention, creation and revolution.

Thou shalt love . . .

Christian morality is, in fact, no more than the logical development of a single commandment: thou shalt love with the very love of God. It is difficult, no doubt, to say exactly what our duty with regard to charity is, and morality too often develops on a purely negative plane. It is much simpler, in effect, to say what must not be done than to say how far we ought to go in the direction of love. That is natural. There are binding laws like barriers, as a matter of course: thou shalt not steal, thou shalt not lie. That is simple, and valid for all times and all places; the path to be followed is clearly visible. But the positive side: thou shalt love thy neighbour, what shades of meaning that admits of, what delicacy, what ingenuity! What new horizons this commandment opens up before our eyes, since it remains a strict obligation at all times and in all places.

The scene of the Last Judgment

If you have any doubt about that, read again the passage in the Gospel which describes the Last Judgment:

> When the Son of Man comes in his glory, and all the angels with him, he will sit down upon the throne of his glory, and all nations will be gathered in his presence, where he will divide men one from the other, as the shepherd divides the sheep from the goats; he will set the sheep on his right, and the goats on his left. Then the King will say to those who are on his right hand, Come, you that have received a blessing from my Father, take possession of the kingdom which has been prepared for you since the foundation of the world. For I was hungry, and you gave me food, thirsty, and you gave me drink; I was a stranger, and you brought me home, naked, and you clothed me, sick, and you cared for me, a prisoner, and you came to me. (Matt. 25. 31-37).

And the Master goes on: "Believe me, when you did it to one of the least of my brethren here, you did it to me" (Matt. 25. 40).

This passage brings home to us the crime we all commit too often, the crime of not loving.

A dialogue

Let each man examine himself faithfully before God and ask for strength and understanding to love better, to discover all the capacity for love he has which has not been used in the service of his brethren. To help you in this examination of conscience, read again the conversation in the celebrated film you all know, in which Queen Anne of Austria engages in a dialogue with Vincent de Paul:

The queen, turning towards St Vincent de Paul, says to him: "You're doing too much, M. de Paul." Vincent replied: "I've done so little."

The queen: "You know you've done a great deal, and there will be few at the Day of Judgment who can give an account of days so well-filled as yours."

Vincent (with a gesture of despair): "I have been idle, so terribly idle, ma'am; I have often been slothful."

The queen: "Ah, M. de Paul, we have thought of nothing but pleasure, of our appetite for enjoyment; and but for you these eyes of ours would never have been opened. Tell me, you who have thought of nothing but giving, you who have renounced happiness and power for ever, you who have built better things than vain palaces and idle renown, do you too, on the threshold of death, feel this great emptiness behind you?"

Vincent: "Yes, ma'am; I have done nothing."

The queen: "What do you have to do, then, in one short life, if you are going to do *something*?"

And Vincent replied with this one word, which I leave with you: "MORE."

XX

LEARNING TO LOVE
ALL THE TIME

The mark by which all men will know you
for my disciples will be the love you
bear one another.—Jesus to his apostles (John 13. 35).

CHARITY means loving men with God's own love. Our
Lord made charity towards others the test of our love
for him and the basis of that final test which we call
the Last Judgment. We are apt to think of ourselves
as up to standard in charity, because it seems to us
that we do no harm to anybody. We find it difficult
to grasp that there is a sin against charity, and this
sin has a name: it is called the sin of omission, or,
in the words of Léon Bloy, "the crime of not loving".

The sin of omission

Let us face up to this sin, explore the vast field of
things we should have done and have not thought
about. Are any examples needed?

Think of the social question. If the working classes
are lost to the Church, it is largely because the
Church, in the nineteenth century, did not feel deeply
enough about the terrible distress of the working
classes and the inhuman nature of working conditions.
"If all nominal Christians," Clemenceau said on one
occasion, "were real Christians, there would no longer
be a social question." A sin of omission, a crime of

not loving, the consequences of which now weigh heavily upon us. We must acknowledge it, because it is true; and also to avoid being taken unawares by more distress and more misery in our own twentieth century. Let us think today of that terrible problem of hunger in the world, those underdeveloped countries whose peoples form two-thirds of the human race, and who live at a sub-human level. May yesterday's sin of omission help to open, first our eyes, then our hearts, to this agonizing question which, at this very moment, claims the co-operation of all men of good will.

Other people's points of view

It is always difficult to think of your neighbour, take his troubles to heart and even, to put it still more simply, look at things from his point of view.

In the post-office, a lady in the middle of a queue which was a little too long for her liking was getting impatient. When at last her turn to be served arrived, she said in a most irritable way to the overworked assistant: "I have been waiting at this counter for half an hour." To which the assistant quietly replied: "And I have been standing here for thirty years, madam." It is a matter of one's point of view, a question of perspective. Try to look at things from the other side of the counter, from the other man's point of view: a whole world of considerateness and kindness will open unexpectedly before you.

Then we shall discover the things we can do to make the lives of others a little more pleasant.

"All human misery," says Isabel Rivière, "comes from greed; wretchedness of body from men's refusal to give their goods; wretchedness of soul from men's refusal to give their time and their hearts." Charity, on the other hand, forgets itself and despoils itself for others.

Things you can discover

We carry within ourselves the source of the happiness we have to spread abroad. As disciples of Jesus, we are bound to create light and spread joy and warmth around us. But some imagination is needed. No one in the world will mark out a ready-made path for us. The only thing anyone can do is to indicate the direction and then tell us to go as far as the Lord's commandment takes us: Thou shalt love thy neighbour "with the love of thy whole heart, thy whole soul, and thy whole strength". Once the attention is aroused, there are so many little things which only require thinking about. "There is a whole world of lovable virtues," Fr Poucel has written, "which are practised so quietly that we never know about them."

There are certain ways of doing things, like closing the door when you go out of the room, walking softly so as not to wake one of your neighbours, picking up papers which have fallen to the floor, not throwing stones in the stream after you have drunk from it, treating a child's doll with respect, learning how to accept a proposition without immediately attacking it with a counter-proposal, not making the invalid's temperature rise when you visit him, complimenting the cook who has taken so much trouble at the stove, lending someone a book you will never get back.

Charity is made up of tact. Charity senses what others are wanting and waiting for. Do you remember the first miracle of all that Jesus did at Cana? What gave rise to it was an action on the part of the Blessed Virgin, who had sensed someone's embarrassment.

To such actions our Lord sometimes attaches unexpected and wonderful results. I am thinking of quite a little incident that happened once.

A Brussels parish priest was coming out of his church one day when he noticed one of his non-practising parishioners taking a photograph of his wife and baby in the porch. The priest went up to the group without thinking twice about it and said: "Don't you think that snap would be nicer if you were in it?" Murmurs of appreciation. The priest took the snapshot, handed back the camera and went off. He had scarcely gone a yard or two when he heard footsteps running behind him. He turned round. It was the wife who came up, all out of breath: "Father, my little boy hasn't been christened. Would you baptize him?" Contact had been made. They talked. It turned out that the marriage was not a valid one. One thing led to another. The little boy was baptized, the marriage regularized. The fullness of the Christian religion entered that home as the result of a tiny act of charity thought of on the spot to meet the need of the moment.

The priest who told me this story ended with an

amused smile and said: "And all because of a snap which didn't come out, anyway!"

An enquiry

That was one example among many of charity on the alert. If we could only let ourselves go with this resourceful kind of charity, we should see a big change in ourselves, the people around us and in our homes. To whet your imagination and spur you on to charity in the family circle, I should like to tell you about a remarkable questionnaire which was sent out quite recently to a large number of children in different continents. They were asked to say what they expected from their parents.

To ensure greater sincerity, a promise of absolute secrecy about their identity was given to those who answered the questions. Now, when they were classifying them systematically, the psychologists who had the job of analysing and interpreting this huge pile of answers, found to their astonishment that the ideas expressed by these children, of all races and colours, hardly differed from one to another.

From their replies this list, which is a résumé of their requirements, has been drawn up:

1. Do not quarrel in front of the children.
2. Treat all your children with the same affection.
3. Never lie to a child.
4. Parents must be nice to each other.
5. There should be some sort of comradeship between parents and children.

6. Receive your children's friends in the same way that you welcome your own.
7. Do not scold or punish a child in the presence of other children.
8. Draw attention to your children's good points. Do not emphasize their faults.
9. Always answer their questions.
10. Always show them the same affection and the same good humour.

It is difficult not to respond to an appeal like that.

What a source of peace and happiness it would be if grown-ups agreed unanimously not to fall below the expectations (and the logic) of the children who observe us and judge us.

Charity is a revolutionary force at the very centre of our homes. Give it plenty of room; give it a warm welcome. And remember these words of Bernanos, with which I want to end: "What others expect from us is what God expects from us."

XXI

LEARNING TO LOVE
IN ALL SITUATIONS

For yourselves, brethren, never weary of doing good.—
St Paul to the Thessalonians (2 Thess. 3. 13).

WE have been trying to understand our positive duty
of charity on the plane of social and family life.

We are so self-satisfied that finding fault with ourselves is most difficult. In that respect, we are not a
bit like real saints, who are the first to accuse themselves of their faults. "A saint," said Chesterton, "is
someone who knows he is a sinner." We have not
reached that stage yet. So it is very necessary for us
to make a list of our sins of omission occasionally.

Let us return to the family, then, and see what goes
on every day in the home. How many crimes of non-
loving! What a lot of little things, little in themselves
but great in the spirit that prompts them, we could
do to make the home a happy one. A ray of sunshine
is enough to light up the whole room. There is such
an incredible variety of things to do in order to create
happiness, yet they cost nothing.

Examination of conscience

In a book of the examination-of-conscience type for
the use of people who lack imagination, we find the
following advice:

FOR MEN

Stay at home when you want to go out for a game of cards—put your newspaper down and give your wife a hand—when your children tell you all about school, listen to them—relieve your wife of some of her running about—avoid an argument by saying nothing—remember your wife's birthday and the children's—say the soup is excellent, and if there's too much salt in it, say nothing—ask the opinion of your older children—give your children praise when they have done well—don't talk about something silly the man next door did—when an old man talks about the past, listen to him—do something for someone who has said something nasty about you—when you have had a bit of luck, pass on some of it to a poor man—tell people about something nice one of the neighbours did ...

And so on; but that's enough for the men.

FOR WOMEN

Smile when you're tired and the children are making a row—take an interest in your husband's work—answer your child when he asks why for the twentieth time—put up with your children's friends, especially if they make twice as much noise —speak highly of your husband in front of the children—go and look at the vegetables your husband has planted in the garden—plan surprises for the children—welcome the in-laws on both sides of the family—order the things your husband likes best—go and see a neighbour who is ill—praise someone whose home is well-kept—quickly forget anything which upsets you and smile when you're worn out.

And the anonymous author goes on to give good advice to boys and girls.

FOR YOUNG MEN

Don't make the hall dirty, particularly when it's just been cleaned—offer to do some of the family shopping—go for a walk to town with your father—don't torment your big sister—don't lounge in an armchair when you could be helping your mother—praise the family cooking—don't contradict your father—give your friend a hand with his homework—rope in the boy who has been left out of the game—listen to the sporting exploits of your friends instead of recounting your own—accept the fact that others don't think like us—put your studies at the service of others—keep up a spirit of cheerfulness in the workshop.

FOR GIRLS

Mend your big brother's jacket without saying anything about it—take your mother into your confidence—put up with your brother's teasing—help the maid with the idea of giving her pleasure—when your father is filling his pipe, hand him the matches—be the first to get up in the morning—teach the whole family to sing songs—remember

your brothers' and sisters' birthdays—tell nice
stories at the office—serve the twenty-fifth customer
as obligingly as the first—give some of your wages
to the poor.

Why have I given you these few examples? Merely
to whet your imagination and stir it up a little. We
have a collection of things there worth thinking about,
and, indeed, I dare say you have all thought about
them. And also to illustrate what I was saying to you
in the course of these talks: that charity has a power
of inventiveness, creativeness. There is no need to be
afraid of inventiveness, of doing something original;
we ought to think of all these little things, for each
day's happiness is made up of them.

Apostolic charity

Charity in social life, charity in family life, and now
apostolic charity. What a lot of sins of omission there
are on this plane! How many Christians have never
done anything in the least apostolic, because they are
unconsciously imbued with the idea that they must
save their own souls; everyone must save his own soul:
how then can they be responsible for their neighbour?

Long ago, in the Old Testament, God asked:
"Where is thy brother?" The question is always up
to date. There are sins of omission, grave sins of omission, today, in the apostolic field.

To make sure you know what I mean, let me quote
an extract from an open letter, in a Viennese newspaper, written by a young Austrian Socialist on the

day after his conversion. I hope this disclosure will stimulate you. This is what he wrote:

I have met Christ at the age of twenty-eight. I consider the years which preceded this encounter as wasted. But am I the only one to blame for this waste of time? No one has ever tried to get me interested in Christianity. I have friends and acquaintances, practising Christians, who have full knowledge of everything religion brings to human life, but none of them has ever spoken to me about his faith. Yet everyone knew I was not an adventurer, a libertine, or a mocker whose sarcasms were to be feared. I was simply one of the thousands, one of the millions of young men who are neither good nor bad, who have a vague and erroneous impression of Christianity. Do you know why I had to wait so long before I discovered the truth? Because most of the faithful are too indifferent, too attached to their own comfort, too lazy. They don't bother themselves about their neighbour's soul.

In the face of that poignant appeal, I beg each one of you to meditate on that crime of non-loving which is too often the sign of our apostolic bankruptcy. No; a Christian is not a man who saves his own soul at the expense of others; he is a man who saves his soul by helping, with all his might, to save the world.

We are expected to be the revolutionaries of Christian charity. This is the sign by which God will recognize us, since, when our lives are over, we shall be judged on love. And this is also the sign by which modern man, that practical man who wants facts, who does not want to be put off by words, will recognize us. It is our job, and nobody else's, to give him proof of it.

XXII

LEARNING TO SPEAK TO THE WORLD

> *The spirit he has bestowed on us is not*
> *one which shrinks from danger; it is a*
> *spirit of action ...   Do not blush, then,*
> *for the witness thou bearest to our Lord ...*
> —St Paul to Timothy (2 Tim. 1. 7-8).

Is the apostolate of the laity an innovation of our own times, a new discovery? Yes and no. No, because the apostolate has always been a duty inherent in baptism, and the early Christians understood this so well that they carried the Gospel to the world of their days. The first to proclaim their joy at the discovery of Christ were Roman soldiers, slaves, business men. They it was who carried the Gospel throughout the empire. For the Church is not an abstract reality; the Church was each one of these men and women; the Church is you, me, all of us together. Or, better still, it is Christ, alive and at work in each one of us. It is the duty of each of the faithful, therefore, to be Christ among his brethren, to allow Christ, through him, to continue His existence as the saviour of His brethren. No Christian who restricts himself to the practice of certain virtues and adheres to certain precepts of his own choice is worthy of the name. If you ask point-blank: "What is a Christian?", you get the reply, as likely as not: "He is a man who goes to Mass on Sundays, makes his Easter duties and abstains on Fridays."

127

That is only half a Christian, a dwarfed Christian. The ordinary, normal Christian is the man who, in addition to this, is actively engaged in the salvation of his brethren.

A Christian, therefore an apostle

We must come back to this duty if we want to live up to our true purpose and not be false to our baptism. No one is a Christian for himself alone, and the lesson in the catechism, where the question is asked: "Why did God make you?", must be clearly understood. The reply is: "to know him, love him and serve him ..." Very good, so long as we are under no false impression as to the meaning of that word "serve".

For the full reply is this: "God made us to know him, love him and serve him and to make him known, loved and served." That is what Christianity is, no less. The Church has always known it, but we are apt to forget it.

What is new, on the plane of the apostolate, is the organization of the vast body of the laity in the service of the extension of God's visible kingdom. In this field an immense effort is still needed to exploit the powers which lie dormant there. In every Christian there is a dormant "Christ-power". It must be brought out, strengthened, given its proper setting, given an opportunity to be fully effective. The combined efforts of all the different organizations of the apostolate are aimed at bringing out this latent power and making it yield a hundred per cent return. We are sometimes told that the world is no longer ready to hear the

Christian message. The truth is that we are not ready to carry it to the world. Hidden in the heart of man is an immense longing for God, a hunger and thirst for God. Let there be no doubt about that. From time to time, in spite of all the Iron Curtains, we can see how acute and how agonizing this longing is.

The world's appeal

I have read recently the account given by a school-mistress who escaped from Hungary. In her infants' class, although it was forbidden under severe penalties to utter the name of God, she had this experience:

One day, she asked if anyone would like to come out and recite a little poem, anything they liked. One little girl put up her hand to say a poem which, she said, she recited every night to her grandmother. And the little girl began: "Our Father, who art in heaven, hallowed be thy name ..." She had scarcely begun before all the rest joined in, and the Our Father was said in chorus.

A sharp reminder of a nation's undying faith; a poignant prayer whose very name was unknown to the little girl. Here is an image of the mute appeal which rises from the world around us. It is the Christian's duty to be the witness, not the silent witness, but the faithful witness of Christ's resurrection. It is his duty to speak the words of salvation to those who seek, those who do not know, those who are wandering in the darkness.

"You can't save your soul like you save money," said Péguy. "You can only save it like you lose money, by spending it." This is the lesson the Church wants her children to learn once more. If you receive a call to the apostolate in whatever form, do not harden your hearts but respond to it; for the faith, if it is to live, must be passed on and spread abroad. And the world has still more need of it than you have; if it is to live, it must have reasons for living and hoping. "Today," wrote Saint-Exupéry to a general who was a friend of his, "I am profoundly sad. I am sad for my generation, which is devoid of all human substance. Ah, General, there is only one problem in the whole world: how to give back to human beings a spiritual meaning to life, a concern for spiritual things. IT IS ABSOLUTELY NECESSARY TO TELL PEOPLE ABOUT THIS."

XXIII

LEARNING TO BE UNITED

*We too, all of us, have been baptized
into a single body by the power of a
single spirit . . .*—St Paul to the Corinthians (1 Cor. 12. 13).

A *discovery*

ONE of the happiest signs of our times is a greater
awareness on the part of all members of the Church
that they are members one of another. The sense of
Christian community is stirring in the lay apostolate;
the Church has become more consciously the common-
wealth of priest and people, and there is a recognition
of the fact that our problems have to be thought out
together and a common front raised to meet the attacks
of the same enemy. This is a living illustration of
Cardinal Suhard's words : "The real agent of evangeli-
zation is not the baptized Christian by himself, nor
the priest by himself, but the Christian community."
The basic cell, the unit of measurement in the apostolate is, as everywhere else, a sort of organic compound,
the inseparable priest-layman combination.

No solution of the problems of the apostolate that
fails to take into account this indispensable union of
the priesthood and the laity can be adequate. A
Brussels parish priest, in an article on pastoral matters,
has written that in order to visit his 20,000 parishioners
at the rate of three a day—and that is a high figure—
he would need at least seven years. We must give due

weight to these figures if we are to understand the urgent need for collective effort and the necessity for everybody to be absorbed at all levels into the community apostolate.

The priesthood of the laity

Nowadays the Church asks priests, with particular insistence, to believe in the baptismal grace in their people, to try and see Christ in them and the power of Christ working through them. Just as the priest's true vocation is not to pray instead of the laity and dispense them from prayer, but to pray at the head of the laity, so he must lead them in the apostolate and not carry it out in their place. Of course, he must know where to find his fellow workers.

Let the priest beware of the temptation to say: "I can't find anyone." At first sight and by human standards, it may be true; but faith will tell him that any soul in a state of grace—a child, or a poor old woman—possesses Christ, and may perhaps be just the fellow worker he is looking for to be the starting-point for a full-scale offensive. A single soul will serve as a lever, and if it is true, as St Charles Borromeo says, that "a single soul is a diocese large enough for any bishop", it deserves all the care we can give it.

All Christians, being other Christs, must of necessity be apostles, since Christ was one. The faithful would be making a tragic mistake if they imagined Christ to be the exclusive prototype of the priest, and not of each one of them. Or again, if they thought the apostolate was reserved for a handful of future saints who, by producing a crop of miracles, would dispense them from all further effort. The priest should repeat to everybody these words of the late Apostolic Delegate to England, addressing a meeting of the faithful: "God has no other voice, no other hands, no other feet, but yours, to carry the Gospel to all parts of the world."

The priesthood of the clergy

From the laity the Church expects more than ever a tremendous respect for the priesthood of the clergy. There is always the temptation to see only the human aspect of institutions and their representatives. We all carry our treasure in fragile vessels. No one knows this better than the priest, for he feels the flagrant disproportion between what he is by the grace of God and what he is in himself. God asks you to clarify your vision and see God at work in this man. This is an exercise of faith, and Christ wills it as a consequence of his incarnation. It is God's will to have need of men; God, completely independent, has willed to be dependent in this way. Accept this mediation of the priesthood, which is the mediation of Christ extended into our own lives. Ask God for a wealth of priests of the kind you long for. And offer him your child generously if the call comes to your home. If God pays you the compliment of knocking at your door, do not destroy the seed of a vocation.

Theory is not enough; it must be put into practice. What is wanted are workers who will put their shoulders to the wheel. Ponder these words of one writer: "In our efforts to build a new world we can do without some of the architects and have a few more masons instead." That's the way cathedrals are built —the only way.

The Church and the world

By way of defining our apostolic task, I want to look for a moment at two realities: the Church and the world.

By Church I mean, in the long run, each one of us; for the Church's name is inscribed on us, body and soul.

By world I mean the mass of people around us who know nothing of Christ, or know him less and less.

We must have the courage to look facts in the face.

The world contains 3,000,000,000 people of whom only 500,000,000 belong to the Church.

The world is a mass which, by the mere increase in the birth rate, is getting farther away from Christ at an alarming rate. In less than fifteen years the population of the world has increased by at least 500,000,000. Of this total, 400,000,000 are outside the Church. For each child baptized a Catholic, therefore, there are four who are not. This proportion pinpoints with a new acuteness the problem of the Church's impact on the world.

The leaven in the dough

It gives a new and modern look to the image Christ presented of his Church when he spoke of her as the leaven in the dough.

Leaven : an active ferment which has to penetrate hostile, indifferent, heavy dough and raise it above itself without ever sinking back again, struggle to keep its own identity, and not let itself be destroyed by the dough which bears on it with all its weight.

If the Church is a leaven, the whole question at issue is whether each of us accepts his role of leaven in the world, whether he accepts his task of active fermentation or is content to be a dead weight.

Note that our Lord never promised his disciples that they would be the greater number or the majority of the world's population. He spoke of yeast, and that is not the same thing.

It must be realized that in a Church wholly on the march, everyone must march; in a wholly missionary Church, everyone must be a missionary; in a wholly Catholic Church, everyone must be a Catholic.

So far, unfortunately, not everyone has understood this. Of course, our neighbour should be approached with infinite respect and tact. But this respect and tact should not be carried so far that nothing is said. We must approach others, and we must speak with tact and respect; and that is a very different thing. Christ has commanded us to go out all over the world, preach the Gospel to the whole of creation and put it within people's reach. That is always a possibility; converting them is another matter. All conversions are a mystery of grace and free will. But it is always possible to put the Gospel at the disposal of all, to carry the message to everybody. And that is what we have been commanded to do.

Let us not refuse to give ourselves to God for the salvation of the world.

The apostolate an intrusion?

There is in existence an insidious slogan which is calculated to paralyse all desire for the apostolate in the hearts of even the best of us. According to this slogan, the apostolate is a violation of the conscience of others, an infringement of their right to have their opinions respected. In virtue of this, everyone must be left free to follow the path his conscience dictates and we should refrain from all proselytism.

We should be in danger of impeding the missionary effort of the Church and being false to Christ if we did not examine these false statements more closely.

Of course the individual conscience must always be respected, the unbeliever's as well as the Christian's. The Church expects something more from the faithful than respect for other people's consciences; she claims from them, too, their free allegiance—in conscience. She has no wish to wring from them an unreasoning faith, which would in any case be false to itself. What she wants is that "honest submission of a free man" that Péguy spoke about. And she has no hesitation in saying that, so long as the truth about Christ or the Church is not apparent to the eyes of the unbeliever, he has no right to join her.

But having said that, the Church tells us once again to go and preach the Gospel to all creation. The command is imperative, like the charity of God which inspires it.

Is the apostolate an intrusion?

If so, the words of the Master: "Go out, making disciples of all nations . . ." would be nonsense! If the good faith of the ignorant were the equivalent of theological faith, the very foundations of all the missions would crumble!

Of course, nothing must be done to wound the consciences of others or involve them in violent conflict. But there are "words of life" we have no right to keep to ourselves, even if our neighbour does not suspect the blessedness they contain. In the matter of spiritual works of charity, there are sins of omission graver than any others, and God will judge us for them.

What clearer evidence could there be of our respect for others than the fact that we put before them the truth we live by and the overwhelming joy of it, which they know nothing about? Surely this is the way to respond to the appeal, conscious or unconscious, of those multitudes in search of the truth and groping for it in the darkness?

I use the word "multitudes" advisedly. I will quote just one example. Do you know that during the course of a single year, a large movement concerned with the apostolate in the United States has received, as the result of public advertisements in the principal newspapers offering to supply information on the subject of Catholicism, nearly 300,000 requests for information about the Church?

In the space of eight years, more than two million requests for information have been received and 208,000 people have undergone religious instruction.

These figures show the size of the hungry multitude who cry for bread in the wilderness and on whose behalf the Master says to us what he said, long ago, to the apostles: "It is for you to give them food to eat" (Luke 9. 13).

May God forgive us for our silence!

XXIV

LEARNING TO SUFFER IN HOPE

> *Was it not to be expected that the Christ should undergo these sufferings, and enter so into his glory?*—Luke 24. 26.

The mystery of suffering

No one escapes suffering. It follows us from the cradle to the grave as surely as our shadow follows us on the road. We find it difficult to understand what must certainly be called the mystery of suffering. We should like to live in a world where there was only sunshine, never any shadow. If it were left to us, we should have a world with only two seasons, spring and summer.

Is suffering a heap of dead leaves, a gust of cold wind, sterile, hostile and evil, blowing from no one knows where? You know as well as I do what effect winter has on our woods: those trees which seem lifeless are preparing for the sap to rise again; those dead branches that we cut down make it possible for new branches to come to life. Winter is not death, but the preparation for life. Winter is not the end, but the soil where the foliage of the future is nourished. Winter is not sheer desolation, but a period of waiting, the gloomy path, the darkness before the dawn. In human life suffering is like the hours of darkness, like winter. Its role is indispensable if we want to live a Christian life of full vigour; if we want, as Jesus put it, to bear fruit: "a grain of wheat must fall into the ground and die ... but if it dies, then it yields rich fruit" (John 12. 24-25).

In some obscure way we are aware of that, but explaining it is difficult. You do not try to tell a sick man, racked by fever, that his fever is a sign of conflict and reaction leading to the restoration of his health. When his suffering is excessive, we hold his hand in token of sympathy, we make him understand we are near him, know what he is going through and share it. But words do not help much: at such a time they seem too superficial, too impersonal. Suffering is such a personal thing, so impossible to communicate to others when it touches the very depths of our being. Sometimes we have to wait for the moment to speak.

The poignant scenes of recent catastrophes are still in the minds of all of us. How can we interpret and understand that immense amount of accumulated, heaped-up suffering; those homes broken at a single blow, those lives cut off in full flower? If life is no more than a fleeting existence, if it ends with the grave and knows nothing beyond the grave, we cannot understand.

To a man without faith, suffering is a dark night with no stars. But to the man who believes that life in this world is a preparation for the life to come, the preface and introduction to what is to follow, light begins to shine in the darkness; he realizes that suffering is a difficult road to travel, but that it emerges into the daylight and warmth which await us on the other side of the tomb.

In moments of grief and separation, the human heart realizes so clearly that the love which unites the members of a family is a lasting reality extending beyond this world; that love, if it is real love, cannot die, because love is something of God and God cannot die. The human heart has no difficulty in believing that the dead are more alive than ever and that they are near us, more than ever present in that unseen but real world which surrounds us.

The world invisible

Even on the natural plane, there are invisible realities quite close to us, as we men of the technological age can readily appreciate. Our ancestors would have been astonished if they had been told that the rooms they occupied were full of sound and light and that it was only necessary to press a switch to capture the waves of what is now called radio and TV. You only have to switch on your wireless set to become aware of these realities around us. It is the same with the invisible things of the spirit. You only have to "switch on" your heart, in faith, to capture those unknown waves, to enter that kingdom of ineffable love which "no eye has seen, no ear has heard, no human heart conceived," to enter that kingdom of love and joy which "God has prepared for those who love him" (1 Cor. 2. 9).

The approach of God

But faith goes farther than that; it penetrates more deeply into the mystery of suffering: it makes the discovery that suffering is not a dull and hostile reality, a ghost-like shadow looming over us; it is painful to bear, but fraught with hope, like bringing a baby into the world; it is full of promise of salvation and redemption. Suffering takes on quite a different look once you realize that it is not an impersonal reality, but the presence of God doing mighty things in us and in the world. Faith reveals to us the living love of God which always lies hidden in the heart of pain—a veiled love, certainly, but a personal and direct love.

You know, it is not difficult to believe that God loves us when everything is going the way we want it. But if we are not going to waver when the storm bursts on our boat, we need a really thoroughgoing faith.

And yet, in the hour of our distress, the love of God is more importunate, more all-embracing, than ever. How easily we misunderstand the advances of this paradoxical love! We refuse to yield to these caresses which break us in pieces in order to flood us with grace. We fail to trust in God because our faith is not strong enough to recognize him, at such times, in the often disconcerting disguise he wears. "We believe, O Lord," the apostles cried, "but help our unbelief." That is a confession and an appeal that we might well repeat in our turn.

If the Christian could only view in this light the approach of God in the perplexity of suffering, what a lot of help he could give to his brother, bewildered by trial and cast down by despair. He could give him consolation and strength. Let the Christian go to him quietly and tell him, in the beautiful words of one writer, that "dawn begins at midnight", that God is at work in his aching heart and that, one day, he will understand the miracles that are being worked, unknown to him, in the depths of his heart.

XXV

LEARNING TO SUFFER WITH FAITH

*Everything helps to secure the good
of those who love God.*—St Paul (Rom. 8. 28).

God at work

You who are listening-in, and perhaps suffering some
grievous trial, ponder the full meaning of these words
of Scripture: "Everything helps to secure the good
of those who love God," and understand that "everything" means "everything". That injustice or that in-
jury, that insult or the act of contempt, that obstinate
misunderstanding, that ill-will, that affliction, that
separation, all that gives pain to the heart of man, all
work together for our good; for all these things are in
the hands of God. Have you ever been present at a
surgical operation? Look at this battery of instruments
the surgeon uses; and the nurses, standing round the
patient and handing out such a variety of things. The
doctor uses first one instrument, then another; puts it
down, then takes it up again. Each instrument makes
a wound in its own fashion, but all of them work together for healing, for those successes in the field of
medicine of which the world today is so rightly proud.
God performs operations, too, to free our souls, loosen
our bonds, remove infection, purify our souls and
re-make them into souls worthy of a happiness past all
understanding and beyond their wildest dreams.

Everything helps to secure our good. And "everything" means those who are unfriendly to us and perhaps wish us ill, as well as the friends God places on our path. God guided the wise men to Bethlehem, not only by a friendly star, which lit up the sky expressly for them, but by the directions of the scribes at Jerusalem and the trickery of Herod, who sought to kill Jesus. In the hands of God, Herod, like the star, served the purposes of love, and, when he had played his part to perfection, the Lord foiled his plots and showed the wise men another way. It is always the same God who loves us, and he loves us as much as he loved the three kings.

The instruments in his hands may change. It is always he who deals the cards, and he deals them with sovereign love.

Look at your trials, and those who inflict them on you, with the eye of faith and see, beyond the hostile faces, the clenched fists, the wounding words, the face of him whose love for you is revealing itself through all these actions of his creatures. He asks you to have confidence in him and leave the last word to his love.

We must return again and again to these truths of faith which shine through the night like a lighthouse and throw out such a light in the darkness. You know Rembrandt's pictures in which light and shade are contrasted with each other. Life is like those paintings. There is too much light to doubt God and his love towards men; there is too much shadow to doubt original sin, which came into the world to destroy God's plan, sow the seeds of revolt and usher in the darkness. At high noon, on a summer day, when the sun is shining with all its might, we have no difficulty in believing in its light and warmth. When it is cold and dark, or merely overcast and foggy, we may be tempted to think the sun has disappeared. Nothing of the sort! It is not the sun which has changed, but the earth which is covered in gloom. In the same way, when we are plunged into suffering and grief, we must believe more firmly than ever in the sun of God's love, which is only looking for an opportunity to break through the clouds and drive the fog away.

If we are to clear our gaze constantly and see things as God sees them (and isn't that what faith is: seeing with God's eyes, judging with God's wisdom?) we must always make the effort to see behind appearances, look beyond secondary causes.

Beyond appearances

There is a wonderful little book entitled: *Abandonment to Divine Providence*. The very title is a way of life. In this book, the author, Fr de Caussade, has condensed in a few pages, with no literary pretensions, but a wealth of Christian wisdom, all that is best on this subject in the Christian tradition. Listen for a moment to what he says:

All creatures are living in the hand of God; the senses perceive only the action of the creature, but faith sees the action of God in everything—faith believes that Jesus Christ is alive in everything and operates throughout the whole course of the centuries; faith believes that the briefest moment and the tiniest atom contain a portion of Christ's hidden life and his mysterious action. The action of creatures is a veil concealing the profound mysteries of the divine action. Jesus Christ after his resurrection took his disciples by surprise in his apparitions, he presented himself to them under appearances which disguised him; and as soon as he had revealed himself, he disappeared. This very same Jesus, always living and active, still takes by surprise souls whose faith is not sufficiently pure and penetrating. . . .

Faith is the interpreter of God; without the illumination which it brings, nothing can be understood of the language in which creatures speak to us. That language is a cypher in which nothing is apparent but confusion: it is a thorn-bush from which no one could imagine God speaking. But faith makes us see, as in the case of Moses, the fire of divine charity burning in the midst of the thorns; faith gives us the key to the cypher and enables us to discover in that confusion the marvels of heavenly wisdom. Faith gives a face as of heaven to the whole earth, and by it our hearts are ravished and transported to converse in heaven.[1]

If our faith is of that calibre, the enigma of human suffering will have been resolved in the secret places of our hearts. We shall know that suffering is a secret

[1] J. P. de Caussade, S.J., *Self-Abandonment to Divine Providence*, translated by Algar Thorold, London, Burns & Oates, 1933, Book I chap. 2.

tryst made with man by God; one which he never fails to keep, if only man will learn to wait a little while for him and put his trust in him.

If our faith is of that calibre, we shall find courage, not only to undergo trials, but also (and this is quite a different matter) to accept them, resign ourselves to them with the kind of resignation Mme de Swetchine was speaking of when she said: "Resignation means putting God between your grief and yourself." To put God between your grief and yourself is to put God at the very heart of suffering and to discover an unsuspected meaning in it, a reason for it which makes complete sense of your life.

If our faith is of that calibre, we shall thank God for all the stones encountered on the road, for the desert we had to cross, the wells which ought to have slaked our thirst, but whose waters were so grievously bitter. All that was willed or permitted by God. All that he has weighed up and counted out, with love. The Lord has seen our tears, as pearls of great price, and they shine eternally before his face. It is good to know that, not in order to make us think of ourselves, but to go forward with a light heart, lift up our heads manfully under the storm and recognize that "the time draws near for your deliverance" (Luke 21. 28).

XXVI

LEARNING TO DISCOVER GOD

*Woman, Jesus said to her, why art
thou weeping? For whom art thou
searching?*—John 20. 15.

The meeting in the garden

LET us read again together the words in the Gospel
which tell us of the meeting of Jesus and Mary Magdalen on Easter morning in the garden where the
Master had been buried:

Mary stood without before the tomb, weeping.
And she bent down, still weeping, and looked into
the tomb; and saw two angels clothed in white
sitting there, one at the head, and the other at the
feet, where the body of Jesus had lain. They said
to her, Woman, why art thou weeping? Because
they have carried away my Lord, she said, and I
cannot tell where they have taken him. Saying
this, she turned round, and saw Jesus standing there,
without knowing that it was Jesus. Woman, Jesus
said to her, why art thou weeping? For whom art
thou searching? She supposed that it must be the
gardener, and said to him, If it is thou, Sir, that hast
carried him off, tell me where thou hast put him, and
I will take him away. Jesus said to her, Mary. And
she turned and said to him, Rabboni (which is the

Hebrew for Master). Then Jesus said, Do not cling to me thus; I have not yet gone up to my Father's side. Return to my brethren, and tell them this; I am going up to him who is my Father and your Father, who is my God and your God.

So Mary Magdalen brought news to the disciples, of how she had seen the Lord, and he had spoken thus to her.

Did you notice the question the angels asked her: "Woman, why art thou weeping?" and her reply: "Because they have carried away my Lord, and I cannot tell where they have taken him."

Here is a woman weeping on an empty tomb. She little knows that this empty tomb is the greatest joy of her life and of the lives of all who people the earth.

God in disguise

She is weeping in the presence of him who is her greatest reason for life and hope.

This woman in tears—is she not the very image of our own failure to understand the mystery of suffering? We see only the emptiness, the break-up, the parting, the loss. We see only the reverse of the coin, and, because these things give us pain, we are desolate.

This woman in tears is complaining because they have carried away her Lord and she cannot tell where they have taken him. She wants to find the body in the grave and make sure it is really there. She wants to reduce things to her own standard of measurement, keep them so that she can understand them.

She wants everything to be neat and tidy; she wants the *status quo* back again. She wants to embalm a body and she mourns an absence which, to her, is cruel.

This woman is mourning while God is giving her the greatest joy of her life. But she does not know it yet. Look at Magdalen; and ask yourself if you, too, do not blame God the minute his own thoughts cease to coincide with yours, the moment his ways cease to be your ways.

Mary Magdalen turned round and saw a gardener. It was Jesus who came up to her, but she did not know him. This woman who failed to recognize God in the guise of a gardener—is she not an image of the Christian deceived by God's disguise?

We believe that God can only come to us with great pomp and ceremony, and in circumstances which we think worthy of him. And the Master delights in coming among his people on any and every occasion, dressed in his working clothes. We want God to treat our scheme of things, our conventions, our preconceived ideas with respect. He laughs at our ideas of what is fitting and comes in all sorts of disguises. God hides behind the anonymity of trial and suffering more readily than otherwise, because there he is nearer, more familiar. He can bend down more easily to our misery. Alas, we find it so hard to believe!

The Magdalen was looking for Jesus, a dead Jesus, and the man she met was the living Jesus, the Master of life and death. She was bewildered, but even her bewilderment was full of the triumph of God. The Magdalen was searching for Jesus "without", somewhere in the garden, and she asked: "Tell me where thou hast put him."

A passage from St Bernard

Here is St Bernard's admirable commentary:

We look for God where he is not to be found, or rather we do not look for him where he is chiefly to be found; hence all the confusion, all the delay and a lot of marking time.

Woman, why art thou weeping? For whom art thou searching? You possess him, the one you are searching for, and you do not know it? You have him, and yet you weep? You look for him without, but you have him within. You stand outside the tomb, in tears. Why? Where am I? Why, within you. That is my resting place; I am not dead, but alive for evermore. You yourself, you are my "garden". You did well to call me the gardener. I too, the second Adam, am in charge of a garden, the garden of paradise. My task is to labour at raising a crop of desires in this garden of your soul. What? You have me, you possess me within yourself and do not know me? That is why you seek me without. Well, here I am. I appeared to you without, so that I might bring you back within. It is there, within yourself, that you will find me. . . .

Ah! I am not absent, I am not far away, as you think. I am close at hand. Tell me, what is nearer to anyone than his own heart? Those who find me, find me there, in their hearts. That is where I live.

May the feast of Easter make plain to you the mystery of suffering; may it bring you to the discovery of God under all the disguises he adopts; may it lead you to the discovery that God is living, and living in you. May the certainty of his presence fill your heart to overflowing with strength, courage and joy.

And when it does, the Church asks you, in the name of the Master, not to keep the secret of your faith and joy to yourself; and she repeats to each of us what Jesus said to the Magdalen: "Return to my brethren and tell them. . . ."

Go, do not keep this good news to yourself.

Go, cry out your joy to the world which, if it is to live and triumph over sorrow, has need of this assurance.

XXVII

EASTER MESSAGE

*Why are you seeking one who
is alive, here among the dead?*
—The angels to the holy women (Luke 24. 5).

SOME years ago, an American film, called, I think, *The
World in Darkness,* depicted the following scene:

An archaeologist was excavating in Jerusalem,
mainly in the Calvary area. One day he announced
that he had found the tomb where Jesus was laid,
the tomb of Joseph of Arimathea, and—the tomb was
not empty. He declared that he had found a mummi-
fied corpse in it, and he put it on exhibition. People
came in crowds to see this corpse. Christ had not,
therefore, risen from the dead. The news was carried
by press and radio to the four corners of the earth.
Immediately the world was plunged into indescribable gloom. Everything which spoke of Christ, everything which lived by him, everything which bore his
mark or a trace of his memory was doomed to
disappear. The churches were closed; the cathedrals
demolished; the pictures which portrayed him disappeared from the galleries; monasteries emptied;
missionaries returned home, the cross was torn down
in people's homes.

Finally, when the world, shattered by this immense
seismic shock, was plunged into complete spiritual

darkness, the archaeologist confessed on his death-bed that he had told a lie and that the tomb had been empty.

Whatever the value of the film, it had at least this merit: it made it clear that nothing is more essential to the world than a knowledge of what happened on Easter morning.

Was the tomb empty? Did Christ rise from the dead? That is the whole question.

The decisive question

To the disciples who stood questioning each other on Easter morning, it was the decisive question. It may be put like this:

Have we lived in vain or not?

Have we wasted our lives or not?

Have the three years spent with him been a mad adventure with no future, or not?

Was this Christ whom we followed an impostor or the Son of the living God?

All their lives hung on the answers to those questions.

And the lives of all mankind.

For since that day, ever since that Easter morning, men have taken sides round the empty tomb.

To one side, Christ is dead, and the dead do not come to life.

To the other, Christ is dead, but he is also alive, and from his death has come life.

According to the side one takes, the face of the world is transformed, values change.

If Christ has not risen . . . then . . .

Heaven is closed.

"You are back in your sins."

The world is a kingdom of darkness and death.

If Christ has not risen . . . then . . .

Tear down the cross from the altar, from the church spire, from our homes; tear down the calvaries which the piety of our forefathers erected by the wayside. Tear down the cross, if you can, from your heart. Silence the bells that ring out a lie.

All this is logical, ruthlessly logical.

If Christ has not risen . . . then . . .

All the martyrs who have given their lives for him, from St Stephen down to the martyrs of our own day, have died in vain, and their executioners had the last word.

But if Christ rose on the third day, as he said, then:

Heaven is open, and one of our own kind has entered it in triumph.

The chains of sin are broken.

Our faith is not in vain.

Our most extravagant hopes are legitimate and our greatest loves certain.

If Christ has risen as he said, then:

Let the bells ring out joyously the alleluia of the resurrection.

Kiss the cross of our redemption and lift it proudly on high in our hearts and on our churches.

Then the blood of martyrs becomes the seed of life.

Let us face the future boldly, and whatever agonies the Church has to go through, let her say with Montalembert: "The Church enjoys, after nineteen hundred years, certain victory and vengeance over those who slander her, enslave her or betray her: her vengeance is to pray for them and her victory to survive them."

The faith of the Church

Today the Church gives voice once more to the cry which has echoed down through the ages:

"Brethren, Christ has risen from the dead."

The Church's life springs from that resurrection. The empty tomb gave her birth. All her joy is Easter joy.

This joy I wish you in my turn. What is a bishop but a witness of the resurrection? He it is who bears official testimony of this marvellous fact, attested by miracles and prophesied by the Saviour.

If Christ has risen, life is open to each one of us. We emerge from the darkness into the light. The philosopher Bergson, long before he was a Christian at heart, wrote these words at the end of one of his books:

"Indeed, if we were certain, absolutely certain, of survival after death, we should find it impossible to think of anything else. There would still be pleasures, but they would be dull and colourless, their intensity depending on the amount of attention we gave them. They would fade like the light of our lamps in the morning sunshine.

"Pleasure would be eclipsed by joy."

There is, in fact, a whole world of difference between pleasure and joy. Pleasure is superficial, joy is profound. It is the joy of Easter which the Church today wishes her children. They are sorely in need of it. Man lives by joy even more than he lives by bread. To know that Christ lives is to know, by the same token, that in its struggle with oblivion and death, life will have the last word; to know that winter has been overcome and spring is not far behind.

It is a message of hope the Church has to offer, to give men the courage to go on, looking forward to the return of the risen Lord in all his glory to take his place at the head of the human race which, thanks to him, will have conquered death.

From now on, the glorious risen Lord goes with us on our way, a contemporary of all who come after him, more alive than ever in the depths of their hearts. No one has expressed more clearly the presence of our Lord, in spite of his death, than Père Lacordaire in one of his celebrated sermons at Notre Dame. More than a hundred years later, this cry of faith and love still echoes, more up-to-date than ever. With these words of his I want to end this Easter message of mine :

We search for love all our life, and never find it except in an imperfect form, and that makes our hearts bleed. And even if we found it during our lifetime, what would become of it after death? I would have it that a kindly prayer followed us beyond this world, a pious memory still pronounced our name; but soon earth and heaven have turned round once more, oblivion descends and silence covers us. No ethereal breeze of love wafts gently from a distant shore to our tomb. It is over; it is over at last, and that is the story of human love.

I am wrong, gentlemen; there is one man whose tomb is guarded by love. There is one man whose grave is not merely glorious, as the prophet says, but whose sepulchre is beloved. There is a man whose ashes, after eighteen hundred years, have not grown cold; who is born again each day in the thoughts of a multitude without number; who is visited in his crib by shepherds and kings who vie with each other to bring him gifts of gold, frankincense and myrrh. There is one man whose footsteps are followed by a substantial proportion of mankind without ever tiring, and, although he has disappeared from view, he is followed by this multitude in all the places of his former pilgrimage; on his mother's knees, by the lakeside, on the mountaintop, along the valley paths, under the shade of the olive trees, in the secret places of the wilderness. There is one man, dead and buried, who is watched when he sleeps and wakes again, whose every word still echoes and produces more than love, produces virtues which are the fruit of love. There is a man who has hung for hundreds of years on a gibbet, and millions of worshippers take him down each day from the throne of his execution and throw themselves on their knees before him, prostrating themselves, without embarrassment, as low as they can; and there, on the ground, they kiss his bleeding feet with indescribable ardour.

There is one man, scourged, put to death, crucified, who, after an unspeakable passion, rose again from death and shame and took his place in the glory of a love which never fails, which finds in him peace, honour, joy to the point of ecstasy. There is one man pursued in torture and death by an implacable hatred and who, when he asks for apostles and martyrs from all those who came after him, finds them in every generation. Finally, there is one man, and only one, who established his love on earth, and that man is you, O Jesus! You who have deigned to baptize me, anoint me, ordain me in your love and whose very name pierces my breast at this moment and draws from it those accents which stir my very being and which I did not know I was capable of.